C000050170

HOW TO
LIVE YOUR BEST LIFE

MARIA HATZISTEFANIS

HOW TO
LIVE YOUR BEST LIFE

TRANSFORM YOUR MINDSET
AND MANIFEST REAL SUCCESS

EBURY
PRESS

Published in 2021 by Ebury Press, an imprint of Ebury Publishing,
20 Vauxhall Bridge Road,
London SW1V 2SA

Ebury Press is part of the Penguin Random House group of
companies whose addresses can be found at
global.penguinrandomhouse.com

This edition published by Ebury Press in 2021

www.penguin.co.uk

A CIP catalogue record for this book is available from
the British Library

ISBN 9781529148459

Typeset in 11/14.25 pt Avenir LT Std
by Integra Software Services Pvt. Ltd, Pondicherry

Printed and bound in Great Britain by Clays Ltd, Elcograf S.p.A.

The authorised representative in the EEA is Penguin Random House
Ireland, Morrison Chambers, 32 Nassau Street, Dublin D02 YH68

Penguin Random House is committed to a sustainable future for
our business, our readers and our planet. This book is made from
Forest Stewardship Council® certified paper.

Contents

Introduction:
Are You Happy?

2 December 2019. I am heading to the 2019 Fashion Awards. It is one of *the* fashion events of the year. It is way up there in the 'see and be seen' stakes, kind of like the Met Ball crossed with the Oscars but with actual royals (as opposed to people who just play them in movies) sitting in the front row. For years I watched from afar, following the winner announcements on Twitter, searching for the red-carpet looks in the press the next day and wishing I'd been there ... not only to breathe the same air as the greatest design names in the universe, but also to witness the drama that only a room full of wildly off-centre fashion geniuses can create: the heartbreakingly beautiful McQueen inmemoriam tribute by Nick Knight and Björk, or when Vivienne Westwood apparently did an endearingly loopy hour-long acceptance speech, or when model Karen Elson fell headfirst off the six-foot-high stage, taking half the set with her. I'd even have been happy to be there in one of the few years where seemingly nothing crazy happened. I just wanted to be part of the scene I loved.

As a teen back in the day, sticking magazine tears on my mood board of dreams, getting an invite to this sort of event was a top-five item on my list of 'when I make it' stuff. Now, here I am in 2019, and I am not only going to the event, but for the fourth year running I am hosting my own table! It is the 'dream come true bonus deluxe edition' of my fantasies – teenage me would be choking on her Diet Coke. This year I truly feel I have made it. I have some amazing guests with me: designers, VIPs and top models. I arrive on the red carpet after an intense afternoon of glamming. I have had my hair and makeup done to perfection and I am wearing a stunning cream-coloured David Koma jumpsuit with feathers. I look like a million dollars and the popping flashbulbs, as I make my way past the ranks of photographers, are a validation ... 'Maria, over here ... One more, Maria ... Maria, Maria, Maria.' They are still shouting my name as I make my way into the baroque splendour of the Royal Albert Hall to greet my guests and take a seat at my table.

If the red carpet is exciting then, once inside the Albert Hall, the glamour is off the scale. The huge circular floor and tiered boxes throng with the impossibly beautiful and charismatic inhabitants of Planet Fashion. As the lights dim and the show begins, a jaw-dropping roll call of celebrities and design superstars takes to the stage. Yet among all this glamour and excitement, my mind is elsewhere.

I spend the whole evening in my head going through something that has been bothering me at work: a work-related deal that I have been working on for six months has fallen through. I just found out this morning. I am upset, angry and disappointed with myself. My team has put their heart and soul into the project, and we have all been working non-stop to make this happen and keep it on track through the ups and downs, which have been many to say the least. Every deal has its tricky moments but this one has been a roller coaster, one day thinking it would go ahead, then the next convinced it was dead in the water. Everybody worked incredibly hard on it but, as ever, being the boss always involves an extra layer of pressure. After all, the buck stops with me. I had been keeping it all together for my team, keeping them motivated and working on the deal while I was absorbing all the punches from this and the other daily dramas of running my own business.

So, I turn up to the awards with all of that front and centre in my mind, which is understandable – it is still very raw. It is particularly devastating to lose the deal but, as I sit at my table on one of the biggest nights of the year, so incredibly lucky, should I really be rehashing every moment instead of enjoying the night? As the champagne flows I am busy quizzing myself. Has it been a total waste of time? Should we have stopped the process when I saw some red flags? Has my 'Make It Happen' attitude actually worked against me this time? Did I push it way past the point when I should have cut our losses and bailed? I fake another smile as I wonder how I will tell my staff we have all just wasted our time.

Although there is nothing I can do to change it, I sit there distracted, not enjoying myself in the slightest, stewing on the bad news. I can't wait to go back home, get to bed, and slot back into my regular routine so I can deal with my work issues. The awards end; everyone is off to after-shows, bars and penthouse parties but I just go back home, relieved I don't have to pretend I am having fun any more. As the car door closes, I sink back in to my seat and breathe a sigh of relief. It's as though the entire evening has been an annoyance and only now can I be fully in my head with no one to interrupt me and my doom-laden thoughts.

Happiness is an inside job. If you had seen me that night you would have thought from external appearances that I must be the luckiest, happiest, most content person in the world. But in my head, I was living a different story. I felt deflated, disappointed, demotivated and like a failure. It didn't matter how I looked or where I was or who I had around me. I was living the story that was in my mind: a story of worry, anxiety and fear. I wasn't living in the moment.

Now, you may think that was a perfectly understandable state of mind. It was a huge potential deal; we worked hard and it was a smack in the face when it all fell through. It would be playing on anyone's mind if that happened to them ... but let us not forget the other side of this. I was at the biggest fashion event of the year. I should have been 'there' and not stuck in my head. I should have been networking, being the best of hosts to my guests, making new friendships and making connections that could lead to bigger and better deals in the future. Instead, I was in a pity party in my head. Everything I went through in my mind that night could have waited ... I wasted my time, my energy and my chances by pouring fuel on the fire of my own disappointment.

I am a very goal-oriented person. Nothing makes me happier than working towards a goal and achieving it, and I have always had goals in my life: goals for the type of job I wanted to do, the type of partner I wanted to have, the type of life I wanted to live. I built this imaginary mood board in my head with the expectation that when I somehow achieved all of these goals, I would arrive at my final destination ... a destination called 'Happy Town'. Population: me. Amazingly, one day, I got there. The journey, although exciting, wasn't the one I had expected or predicted, there were ups and downs, there were good times and bad, but somehow, along the way, I ticked off every single one of those mood board must-haves and finally reached the magical borders of Happy Town. And you know what? I was happy. I had proved them all wrong, I had only gone and done it! Yes! Go me!

There is no denying that the buzz I got from achieving those goals was exhilarating, but (yes, as you predicted, there is a 'but') it was fleeting. It was a momentary thing. Happy Town dissolved into the mist. It seemed so real, and for a while it was real, but in the cold light of day when the excitement died down, it was as though I had dreamed it. I'd done everything and achieved everything I aimed to do … but did that protect me from feeling unhappy, sad or upset? I think you know the answer to that.

We live in times of confusion, self-doubt and constant movement, and more often than not this state of being is self-inflicted. Yes, you are your own worst enemy. I know I am mine. You may have picked up this book because you are going through a phase in your life where you feel unsettled, frazzled and in need of peace and focus … either that or you are killing time in a bookshop and liked the cover. Either way, know that you are not alone. I've been there, and along the way I got my life into focus and, while doing that, I bought some really good books. So keep reading, as I want to share with you some of the things I have learned while dancing along the edge of my own personal abyss: the ideas and ways of looking at myself and the world that helped me and I hope will help you get grounded, calm and happy within yourself. I learned this stuff the hard way, so whether like me you are chasing success or just want to feel good in your own skin, this book will give you the boost you need to get on with life and work in the most spiritual way.

In short, goals are great, but are you happy?

Just to be clear, I know that is a sweeping statement. What 'Happy Town' looks like in your world is up to you, but I do know that getting to it can be a journey full of twists and turns. I've travelled the road and I've got the map. This book is not the ultimate guide to happiness but a field guide of my personal and practical tips for how to address the different challenges that we may face. This is the stuff that worked for me, and brought me back to a state of being content with myself and feeling positive and happy about the present and future. I hope through my words I am able to help you find your own way to your destination.

We all have good days and bad days and that's OK because you are not alone. You may feel there is no light at the end of the tunnel, but there is and I see you!

Life is a journey. That phrase sounds corny, I know, but the overuse is down to the truth. In fact, when I was talking about the need for a destination – about reaching the magical candy-coloured 'Happy Town', population: me – that was simplistic. There is no final destination: it's a series of pin drops on the great Google map of life. 'Life is a journey', for sure, but recently I've found it more useful to consider it like a road movie – you have a destination in mind in scene one, but it is what happens along the way that is the really interesting bit ... the rest stops, the seedy motels, the epic scenery, the soundtrack, the hitch-hikers you pick up, the rip-offs, the good guys and the bad guys, the car you get to drive, the freedom and the boredom, the bonds you make and break, the friendships, the sunsets, the love you win and lose. (Wow, I want to watch *Thelma & Louise* so bad right now!) My point is that, as so often happens in these stories, the journey changes you, and the destination you thought you wanted at the start perhaps isn't the place you need or want to end up in. And besides, when you get there that isn't the end ... you'll sit for a while and catch your breath, but before long you'll be off on another journey. It's a long, endless road, so you need to know how to enjoy the ride.

In my own personal movie there have been plenty of times that instead of being the one driving the open-top Cadillac, I felt like I was trussed up in the trunk. I've been through good times and bad times. I've been in healthy and happy relationships, and in toxic and unhealthy ones. I've trusted people in my professional and personal life and had that trust repaid, only to find my next encounter left me hurt and disappointed.

There are only so many hits you can take, and when I found myself on the ropes for the umpteenth time, I took my own advice and tried to look for a different solution. When I began looking for answers in what, for simplicity's sake, I am going to call 'the spiritual world', I found that was the thing that saved me from going insane. It showed me there is light at the end of the tunnel, and the place at the end of the tunnel is not always what you expect. While I am always learning to face new challenges and finding new ways to cope with life's curveballs, I do believe that what I have learned so far can help you to find some answers too. I want this book to be the beginning of your own spiritual journey, and I want to send you off with a few useful tools, a bit of local knowledge and some clear directions to get you started on the road to finding your own spiritual awareness.

So, having decided to put all that I have learned in a book, I had to ask myself, 'Who is this book for?' Well, it's for you, of course. As I say, I don't know how you have come to be reading this, but hopefully there is a pearl or two of wisdom waiting here for you, as well as the odd peek into the predictably insane life of the beauty business, which at times drives me crazy but which I love to the core. I have tried to be as practical as I can in offering advice that you can use whenever you find yourself lost. If you spend a lot of time in your head and you feel overwhelmed in life and business. If you don't feel as powerful as you know you could and people around you affect your energy and don't get you; if you compare yourself to others and feel bad; if you want to be happy, successful and follow your passion but something or someone is blocking you; if you feel others control your happiness and you feel guilty about putting yourself first; if you are suffering from work-related stress, dealing with insecurity or just feeling generally defeated by life ... or even (God help you!) if it's all of the above, then read on.

Whatever challenges you face, I hope that this book will help you to see them from a different point of view: to be a master of your happiness and raise your energetic vibe so you can have more joy and happiness in your life. I want to help you to let go of the external factors defining your happiness now and hand you the controls. I have condensed years of my own work and self-discovery into a practical guide with everything you need to know.

What I plan to do with this book is analyse what is blocking and draining your energy and ultimately preventing you from being successful and happy, and then look at the tools and strategies that can help you align with your highest self and be the person that you want to be. I wrote this to fire you up, and my goal ... no, our goal ... should be that, by the time you have finished this book, you will be well on the way to living your best life. I want to help you live a life in which you are truly alive, free and full of sparkle. The time is now.

If you have read my books before, you know how I roll. As I always do, I will share my learnings with you so you can enjoy your journey too, but I have approached this book a bit differently in that I am writing this book in real time. Not only am I bringing you my learnings from life, relationships and business, but I am constantly analysing and updating my behaviours as I write, coming up with strategies to face issues while sharing it all with you. Writing this book has already helped me understand myself better, and I know that I will come back and re-read the book, and use it as a quick reminder of how to deal with challenging situations, get out of my head and live in the moment.

The other thing you will find (which I have been told is very 'me') is my need to demystify spirituality and talk about it in a practical way. I want real solutions to real situations (and I am sure you want that too), but even I found that it's sometimes hard to find the answer with logic. My default position was always to try and fix things, and when they didn't get fixed I'd get stressed, upset and obsessed, and I'd force a solution. Unlearning this was key. What if you were to take a step back and trust your gut or, as you would say in spiritual terms, 'let the universe guide you'? When you are at that crossroads and you don't know which way to go with a job, your career, relationship or which colour of the new Bottega shoe to invest in, spirituality can give us answers to everyday problems in a more elevated way (and that Bottega shoe colour choice can be a major problem, believe me – you *cannot* be seen wearing the wrong one). What I'm saying is that sometimes you can't solve a problem at a problem's level, and becoming a lot more spiritual has helped me navigate and better understand my relationships at work, with my family, with the world and, crucially, my relationship with myself.

With this book, I am on a mission to help everyone out there to realise one thing. That happiness lies within us. It is 100 per cent down to us to be happy and no one else is in control of our happiness. And if we are leaving our happiness in the hands of another person, or situation, or in material wealth, we are doing something wrong. It's time to reset, adjust and take the power back.

Fasten your seatbelts and let's go on this spiritual journey together!

Love & Light

x Maria

1

Don't Follow Me, I'm Lost Too

31 December 2019. Just as I have every year, I am sitting down to write my New Year's resolutions. It's something I look forward to – a great excuse to focus on the exciting prospects a new year can bring and make a list. I like lists, I am a list geek ... so sue me. Every New Year's Eve since I was a child I have sat and whittled down the tons of ideas, plans and goals I have been mulling over ... enough to keep me going not just for the year but for another five years. And so, with the fireworks and revellers loudly ringing in a new decade outside my window, I take out my pen and select a fresh page in my Moleskin notebook. But something strange is happening. I can't come up with anything.

Hold on, turn the TV off ... OK now. There, that's better. Now, let's go. World domination, here we come. Just write the ideas down. The pen hovers ... I thought I had something, but no. Wasn't there a thing I thought of, about, y'know ... the thing ... erm ... Nope.

This time, I was numb. I didn't have anything.

What was happening? I felt uninspired, unmotivated. I had nothing. I decided to look back at the past year and analyse it a bit. What worked, what didn't? What raised my vibe, what lowered my vibe? What had inspired me and could I recapture that feeling?

So instead of my usual list of New Year's resolutions I began to write down a quick 'Year in the Life of Maria' retrospective. Then I read it back. Yeah, OK, no big surprises. I already knew it had been a challenging year. My business had a lot of ups and downs, people I trusted let me down, I had moments of feeling confused, without a purpose and deflated, but surely it wasn't all bad? There were parties, fashion weeks, photo shoots and several Bottega Veneta items had found their way in to my wardrobe somehow. I looked at my camera roll to see if I was missing something. Scrolling through the months of 2019, I found that instead of the usual pictures from high-vibe events, pics of me hanging out with interesting people and exciting appearances and selfies with Kendall Jenner, I could find nothing. Well, nothing that excited me. Nothing that cancelled out the depressing list of 'bad year' stuff I'd written in my notebook. So, I guess it wasn't all in my mind. It must have been a bad year after all. Somehow, I had let the bad things take over and unwittingly grind me down until now, here I was, with no spark left, no inspiration, no resolutions. I was numb.

Once that had sunk in, I started to look deeper into the situation. Who or what was responsible for me not enjoying this past year? Was it my work, my family, my friends, my team? It must be something. Well, whatever it is I tell you one thing, it's embarrassing. Here I am, Mrs Positivity, writing books and encouraging others to take opportunities and live life to the fullest and I can't even follow my own advice. I couldn't care less about success and I certainly was not Making It Happen.

Looking back at the year in more detail, I realised that from early on I had been facing the usual challenges in a reactive, low-vibe, victim mode. In business, as in life, there will always be challenges, and this year had started off with a couple of crackers and hadn't really let up. I had gritted my teeth and dived into them head first and had, I realised, been channelling all my energy and attention into solving one thing after another and neglecting to live my life. As my business grew and I overstretched myself, it became seemingly all-important. I had to be honest with myself that over the past year the tipping point had been reached ...

and it had tipped the wrong way. As I investigated further, flicking through my calendar, I realised (and was quite frankly shocked to see) that on several occasions I had been so drawn into the various day-to-day dramas that swirl around every business that I had said no to a lot of opportunities. Looking back on it now, I realised that saying yes could have led to a more exciting, more fulfilling year. It broke my heart to see the 'thanks, but no thanks' emails and messages I'd sent through the previous 12 months. Trips that I said no to, events that I didn't attend, coffee catchups I didn't set up. I was shocked when I looked at the life I could have lived. In an alternate dimension there was a Maria living her best life, writing a New Year's resolution list full of buzzing optimism and world-beating business ideas. Meanwhile, in reality, I was looking in a mirror at someone who might as well have been living under a rock.

This New Year's Eve was an important moment. I had spent a year with my body being in one place and my mind somewhere else. And now, on what is traditionally the most optimistic night of the year, I had faced up to the awful truth. I wasn't aligned or connected with myself. I was unhappy, miserable and not fun to be around. How did I end up here? And, more importantly, how can I snap out of it? I needed to get back to myself, get organised, get disciplined, get in the moment. Easy, right? I've written two books that pretty much cover all this, I just need to follow my own advice. I have the tools, I have the skills. Let's make a list (told you): take up meditation, plan self-care, exercise to release those endorphins and clear my head, take a break. I know all the tools; I have talked about them and used them in the past. The tools were all there. What was different? Was I resisting something? Was I not being honest with myself? Sometimes you just don't realise you are falling into the old patterns. You know how to fix a problem but first you have to admit to yourself that you have one. It's standard stuff. So what was my problem? Where did I go wrong?

Here, for your enjoyment, is my life in a day: wake up (early), wake up properly (espresso), meditation and/or workout, have breakfast, head to work (attempt to block out hellish London commute), arrive at work, team meetings, client meetings, challenges, desk lunch and emails, store visits, more meetings, more challenges, head home (attempt to block out hellish London commute), collapse from exhaustion on sofa, stare at most watched programme on Netflix (i.e. husband scrolling through the menu), doze off, spill tea on cushions, go to bed. Repeat.

There are the odd variations, a fashion show here, a product launch there, a homework dilemma or family crisis (usually involving school football kits and their mysterious whereabouts), but as a rule, I've been following the same routine since I started my business. Along the way, I built two global beauty brands, Rodial and NIP+FAB, I've launched some amazing products, I've built loyal teams and, when my life does deviate from the norm, it can be pretty exciting. I've met some amazing people and visited some incredible places. It's a balance of normal life and glamour that on paper seems to be a dream combo. For someone looking in on my life, it seems that it's a smooth ride.

Well, not quite. There is always something that throws things off-balance. A new product that doesn't arrive on time and we have to scrap all marketing activities and write off all costs. A hiring spree to grow the business and then losing a few accounts and being left with tons of staff and not enough work. A difficult distributor that brings drama to every conversation and causes friction and unease within the team. A team member who thinks they are always right and is causing ripples in the business. A competitor that steals your products and ideas and undercuts you with more success. You get the vibe. And the constant voice in your head that, regardless how far you've come, keeps on coming back, second-guessing your every move, making you doubt yourself and your decisions.

Let's do another jaunt back in time. Here's me in my late teens/early twenties. I'm making a mood board of all the things I think make happiness and success. It's got fancy houses, clothes, a beautiful family – pictures from magazines that seem to sum up the surface of happiness. I had built a picture in my mind that achieving success in my professional and personal life and surrounding myself with material goods were the secret to eternal happiness … and nothing about the standard picture of happiness has changed since then.

When I look at what we are exposed to over social media and, well, just life in general I can't see how that 20-year-old would think any different today. Twenty-year-old me would probably be a fan of someone like Selena Gomez. I'm sure of it, in fact, because 'today' me is a big fan of her music and I have been following her journey for years. As I write, she is in her late twenties, one of the most successful artists of our age, she has the looks, fame and money *and* she used to date Justin Bieber. She's reached a level of success that would take people decades, if ever, to get to. Isn't she the luckiest person in the world? Any 20-year-old would certainly think so, and would idolise her, but as is often the case, things are not what they seem. She's been very open about her emotional struggles and anxiety and how she has taken meditation courses and sought therapy. As far as the world outside is concerned, she has achieved everything any 20-plus-year-old could ever hope to accomplish in their lives. Yet it seems even she came to the moment where she had to stop and ask herself: 'Am I happy?'

So, I looked at the research, I read the books and attempted to find an answer to my fundamental question: 'What is happiness?'

Here we go: happiness is defined as an electrifying and elusive state. More than just a positive mood, happiness is a state of wellbeing achieved by living a good life with a sense of meaning and contentment. So now we know.

All pretty straightforward right? By that definition I'd made it ... I'd got to number one on the happiness list ... but I am here to tell you that while achieving success brings you a sense of achievement and momentary feeling of happiness, success is not the be-all and end-all of happiness. This would be a pretty short book if it was.

So, my research was bearing fruit. I couldn't argue that I hadn't achieved success, but I needed to find a way to make those moments last and be in a state of general contentment, regardless of where I was on my mission in life. I started looking in other directions to find out how to get to a state of being content and at peace with myself, even when the pressure is on. How do I enjoy what I have? That's when I discovered spirituality.

And 'spirituality' is going to need some explaining before we continue.

Here is my definition: spirituality is being concerned with the human spirit or soul as opposed to material or physical things. A spiritual person is someone whose highest priority is to be loving to themselves and others, and knows that we are all connected. Spiritual values include truth, righteousness, peace, love and non-violence.

That all sounds very worthy, I know, but I need a version of spirituality that fits me, while still wanting to achieve my goals and be productive and creative. I decided to research spiritual elements that I can incorporate into my daily life in a practical way.

But how do you go from being a hardcore, success-obsessed high achiever to becoming more spiritual? Where do you even start? Hanging out with monks in Cambodia, joining Madonna on the Kabbalah trail, only drinking water cleansed by healing crystals, jade eggs? I have tried (almost) all in an attempt to find what works for me. I've read books, watched YouTube videos, listened to podcasts, hugged trees, eaten kale ... the whole lot. I have ramped up on my meditation, tried therapy and started to look at moon astrology.

I know I am not on this journey alone. It is a well-worn road. A lot of well-known public figures have taken on spirituality as a way to improve their lives. At age 19, Steve Jobs took a trip to India where he learned about Buddhism and reached a state of zen through meditation. When he came back from India, so the legend goes, he was in such an elevated state he started creating the Apple computer. That's when his success began, and even after his success he remained in touch with his spirituality by meditating daily, despite his busy schedule. It helped him to maintain the clarity to stay focused on his goal rather than wasting attention on unimportant things.

One of Steve Jobs' mantras was 'focus & simplicity'. It means that simpler can be harder than complex, and that is evident in all of Apple's design. The products are all deceptively simple: beautiful solutions to complex problems. At times we all overcomplicate our lives when the solution is simple and is right there. Connecting with spirituality can allow us to find the simple solution, to say no to one thousand things so we can concentrate on that one thing that is really important.

I know business; I am not a healer, guru or spiritual leader. However, I did my research to be able to better understand myself and the patterns in my life that were taking me away from being content and at peace with myself. First, I looked at what I was doing when I was on autopilot. What were my patterns? Overthinking and not 'being in the moment' were the first things I decided I had to tackle. The amount of times I would be in the middle of a beautiful dinner but not enjoying a minute of it because I was re-running a difficult conversation with an employee, or 'what I should have said' in a client meeting. Reading about the spiritual approach made me realise that most of the time my body was in one place and my mind was somewhere else ... and it wasn't just work-related. The one thing I seemed to come back to again and again was obsessing over having my extended family over for dinner and fearing they would not get along. The hours I spent worrying about that (most of the time I was right to worry, but that's not the point); I had to learn to take it easy and chill out! Once I started thinking about it, I could see countless times when I had overthought a situation, worried to death about it and ended up not getting the best out of it for anyone, let alone myself.

It was time to make a list! Get out of my comfort zone, shake up my routines and learn how to raise my vibe ... all went on the list. How to deal with challenging clients and meetings but within my boundaries … also on the list. One thing after another went down on that list – all of them were things I thought I had under control but now I realised were things that had been controlling me.

Step one was already underway. I was on the road to identifying the patterns that were affecting my contentment, peace and, yes, happiness! Step two was to look into the toolbox that I already had and develop specific strategies to cope with stress, anxiety, uneasiness and low vibes, and use the things I had learned to turn myself around and operate in a high-vibe state.

I am writing this book in real time, so I'm analysing my behaviours and coming up with strategies to face them while sharing these with you. And as I travel through this journey, I will meet and speak to gurus and spiritual teachers, and I'll also connect with my Instagram community via @mrsrodial, another tool to help me learn about spiritual ways to deal with everyday problems and find the path to happiness.

How to Live Your Best Life Secret #1

10 signs that you live in your head

Research has shown that we are at our happiest when our thoughts and actions are aligned. How you spend your day doesn't tell you how happy you are. So next time you are stuck in traffic, talking to someone or eating lunch, take note of what you see, hear and feel in the moment. Below is a checklist to question whether you are living in the moment or whether you need to shift your perspective:

1. Do you dread the day ahead? You have nothing you are looking forward to. You have days where you don't feel excited or inspired about what's coming up.
2. Is your daily routine predictable? You know exactly how your day will go, not just today, but in a month's time. It will be exactly the same.
3. Do you do things without thinking? You function on autopilot and don't take the time to ask yourself why you are doing the things you are doing.
4. Do you constantly check your phone for updates? You scroll down your social media feed at any opportunity without looking for anything specific.
5. Are you always deep in your thoughts? You are constantly thinking about things that are not happening while you are doing something else.

6. Do you have a difficult time remembering small things? You are not in the moment and you can't even remember any of your basic activities like driving, what you had for lunch or what someone said to you.

7. Do you find it difficult to let go? You are stuck in a career, friend group, place or situation that doesn't serve you or inspire you any more.

8. Are you not making progress on your goals? Days, weeks and months go by and nothing changes. You are not focusing on what's important and that brings you down.

9. Do you always say yes? You say yes to things that you know are not right for you just because you'd rather not let others down or rock the boat.

10. Do you believe life could be much better? You know there is a better life to be lived but you feel stuck because of your current situation. You know that you have settled in too many areas of your life and you wish you could have followed a different path.

If you answer YES to most of the above questions, you have picked the right book. Keep reading to get some clarity and direction on how to move away from overthinking and living your life on autopilot, and how to move into an intentional way of living.

2

Get Out
of Your
Comfort
Zone

1 January 2020. After the crisis of confidence I had while setting my New Year's resolutions, I have settled on just one resolution, and that is to simply move away from a mediocre 2019 and look to 2020 as the year to 'Live My Best Life'. No more nine-to-five at work then straight home, no more going to bed at 9.30 to be up at 6am for my meditation/horoscope reading. If I want to go out and stay late, I will. The year 2020 will be when I stop acting as though I live in a high-fashion convent; I want to shake up my routine, shock Mother Superior and kick out the jams. It's time to live a little and have some fun.

Well, that was the plan ... and it started so perfectly. Before January had even managed to get its socks on, I had planned, booked and set off on a little weekend in Paris to rest, recharge, get inspiration and set the tone for the rest of the year. No family, no friends, just me. I needed that time to myself, out of my comfort zone and away from daily distractions, to start the year on the right foot, and it doesn't hurt that my chosen venue for this just so happened to be one of my favourite hotels – the beautiful Sofitel Paris Le Faubourg. It was time to spend a wonderfully indulgent weekend on myself, and I did not hold back.

My mornings were spent lounging in a fluffy white bathrobe sipping espresso, before enjoying a leisurely breakfast. I might go for a walk through the winding backstreets of Le Marais or the manicured gardens at the Palais Royale, or spend some time getting to know Degas, Manet and Renoir at the Musée d'Orsay, or sit by the banks of the Seine and gaze wistfully up at the Sacré-Coeur, have lunch in a hidden café, do a bit of shopping ... Basically I could do anything I liked, which included spending most of the day imagining myself as a Parisian film star from the

1960s. No schedule, no plans. I could do what I wanted to do when I wanted to do it and no one was judging. I got so much inspiration from this trip and, as the muse struck me, I would whip out my iPad and jot down ideas and notes. In fact, a large part of this book was written on that trip. The weight lifted from me as I took a step back from my everyday reality of work and family responsibilities, put some space between me and anything that felt heavy, and gave myself the freedom to be creative.

Needless to say, I came back home feeling elevated and refreshed, with lots of positive high vibes, and I promised myself I would not slip back into my old 2019 pattern of All Work No Play Makes Maria a Dull Girl. I would try to find times during the workday and the weekend to get myself out of my comfort zone and keep hold of that freeing, inspired feeling. It doesn't mean that I need to travel to Paris every weekend … although, come to think of it, that would be a great thing to do! I could achieve the same result by shaking up my morning routine and going to a new coffee shop around the corner from my office, or by saying yes to an invite that I would have declined in the past, or by going to bed an hour later and enjoying a night out. The point is to do whatever you need, and I was determined to get out of my comfort zone, break the patterns and try something new as often as I could. I started 2020 on the right foot and was ready for world domination.

As if on cue, the next three months were packed with exciting trips and launches, but instead of approaching them with my 2019 head on – the one which would have been anxiously fussing over agendas and micro-managing the detail – I strode into town with my 2020 head held high. Cover the detail, yes, but then roll with the good times! And after a flurry of events in London and New York, followed by a book launch during New York Fashion Week at the chicest of venues (Le Coucou at 11 Howard Hotel), then, on the well-trodden path of fashion week stops, I finally return to Paris to take over backstage with Rodial at the Coperni fashion show, one of the hottest tickets in town. While I am there, invites to shows just keep on coming: Balmain, Isabel Marant, Redemption, the Carine Roitfeld impossible-to-get-an-invite party. Do you have time to stop by our showroom so we can dress you? The 2020 me says, 'Hell yes I do.' Front-row seats, street-style shoots, professional glam every day at (obviously) my very chic suite at Sofitel Paris Le Faubourg. I can't believe my life right now, and to top it all we are hosting a book launch at the Café Prunier in Paris. Here I am living the life of a superstar and what's more I am enjoying it. My New Year's resolutions are finally coming true. I *am* living my best life. It is 1 March 2020. There are still ten months to go in what is shaping up to be my best year ever. I've got the attitude, I've got the ideas, I've got the look … nothing can stop me now! Nothing!

Then two weeks later, on 16 March, 2020 is cancelled and the world goes on lockdown.

The COVID-19 coronavirus has become a pandemic. The news headlines are difficult to comprehend … they seem to be from the script of a sci-fi-zombie-apocalypse movie but they are not, they are real, and we are really living in these times. Hundreds of thousands of people infected every day, thousands of people are dying, and the predictions are worse. I am in denial, I mean, come on, this is 2020, this doesn't happen in the modern world … this can't be. It's probably just the media making it sound bigger than it is. What else are they going to fill their rolling news schedules with? But the deaths don't stop and after several weeks of uncertainty and speculation the theatres close, the restaurants and bars close and the shops close, so my sales team have nowhere to go, and no one to sell to.

I try to digest it all but I still can't quite compute that this is a real situation. I am clinging on to the idea that this will go away in a week, someone will find it can be cured by eating more pickled beetroot and that'll be that. Just pretend it's not happening ... keep smiling, keep dancing. I am wondering why the office is so busy at lunchtime when I realise it's because there is no lunchtime session at SoulCycle (it's a thing), but here in my bubble of denial I still don't think it'll be long before we all 'get back on our bikes' as it were. Several people in the office are wearing masks and there is much discussion comparing the Hello Kitty ones to the Chanel ones and whether it's going to mean the death of lipstick. Hmm, mask-resistant lipstick? Make a note. Might be worth it, if this is going to last, of course.

I am still in this state of dazed disbelief and semi-denial when the head of operations comes to my office. 'Maria, we need to arrange laptops for everyone to work at home.' I brush it off. I am still expecting the news that it was all an overreaction and we don't have to close after all. 'No, Maria, these are government instructions and we need to close the office within 24 hours as we are a non-essential business.' I am numb. My bubble is dangerously close to bursting. Wait a minute, hold it right there, buster; what do you mean we are non-essential? Is shining, radiant skin non-essential? Are transformational face masks and facelift-grade creams non-essential? Are life-changing concealers non-essential? I'm pretty sure they are top of the list for a lot of people! In times of global strife is there anything more uplifting than a skin-lift foundation? Anything that can give humanity more of a boost than an Intense Booster Drop?

Black humour – if you don't laugh, you'll cry. My denial bubble had burst. There's no getting away from it and the faces of my staff are difficult to ignore. They are all paralysed by fear. So, by the end of that day I had faced the facts and got myself motivated to make it happen. We got the laptops organised, and as I said a teary goodbye to all of my incredible team, I wondered what tomorrow would look like with everyone working from home.

Mostly I expected it to look like someone in pyjamas, watching Netflix, scrolling through their phone and getting annoyed if I sent them an email. I had always had the attitude that if anyone asked me if they could work from home they were basically asking for a holiday, and the odd time the situation had arisen in my team, I usually didn't even bother connecting with the person. I assumed no work was getting done, other than perhaps an in-depth analysis of how long a bath could last or a ten-page report on which pyjamas go best with their sofa. So, with those preconceptions of how working from home functions firmly in my mind, how was I meant to manage a team and run a business? I fully expected no work to be done at all. Last year, we almost went bankrupt and only narrowly escaped. Well, now we were almost certainly going to go under.

Is there a manual on how to manage a team from home during a pandemic? Er ... no. Even Google university couldn't help me now. This is uncharted territory. We are writing history ... or at least making it up as we go along.

The first thing I need to do is come up with some kind of structure for myself and my team's day. Firstly, I need to ensure I connect with all my managers on a daily basis and so I set half-hourly calls, starting from 9am until lunch, then lunch break, then back again to check in, plan and get updates from the various departments.

It felt good to have set some kind of structure and rhythm to the day, and I felt as though I was 'being the boss': keeping everyone on their toes. You can forget the pyjama and Netflix game ... working from home is serious shit! It took a while to get it all working smoothly; there were the inevitable technical challenges, one because someone was staying at their parents' house in the country – great for walks and home cooking, not so good for mobile reception. Or the Zoom meetings where someone can't seem to unmute; screaming babies drown out the call, children run around in the background, cats walk on the keyboard, participants freeze in the middle of an important point, never to be heard from again, not to mention the constant distraction of trying to see what's on everyone's bookshelves. Still, at least no one set themselves on fire, went to the toilet with the camera still on, forgot they weren't wearing trousers or had a naked partner wander in – all actual video conference moments that went viral during the early weeks of lockdown. If this time in isolation has taught us anything, it is video conference etiquette!

So, myself and the team all learned to cope with the new normal and avoid opening the wine before lunch, and soon we were into a great routine. We made sure we had the same call schedule at the same time each day and we quickly got into our flow. And you know what? I felt I was connecting with my teams more than I had connected before. We had a chance to go into more detail than we ever did with the hurly-burly of the office going on around us. Working from home, everyone was calm, dealing with their tasks and seemingly a lot more focused on their job than before. When you commute to work, there is a level of stress that comes with it: delayed trains, crammed buses, running late. And then when you are at the office with people around you, you get involved in conversations, dramas and unnecessary, distracting gossip. By being at home and focusing on the core of your work, the distractions, annoying situations or toxic people that are usually all around you don't have any space or power over you, and you can be the best that you can be. You manage your own energy without distractions.

It's funny that, in January 2020, I promised myself to get out of my comfort zone. I had imagined this would mean being out there a lot more, enjoying life as much as work and moving myself out of rigid routines. As is often the way, that wasn't quite how it worked out, but in March 2020 I discovered a new way to get out of my comfort zone, without even having to move from my own space. When we got this working-from-home thing sorted out and got into a routine, I felt a sense of achievement. Here I was in a situation that I had never faced before, dealing with uncertainty and fear- not just for my business but for my friends, loved ones and, let's face it, the entire world- but I went with my instinct and created a new normal that actually worked! In my first book, *How to Be an Overnight Success*, I talk about how you need a catalyst to get you out of your comfort zone. For me, getting fired was the catalyst to start my business, and now a global pandemic was the catalyst I needed to look at my business and my way of working in a different way.

This time has forced us all to work and connect in different ways and I don't think we will ever go fully back to our old ways. I am not saying we won't ever go back to the office and there are good reasons to have one. You do need face-to-face meetings to connect with the teams, integrate new starters, meet new partners. But now we will think twice before commuting to the other side of town for a meeting: 'How about we Zoom?' In fact, the amazing tech that has helped us through these times can only get better. I imagine that there will be an explosion of new innovations and ideas sparked by so many people thinking about how we have been working recently and finding better and bolder solutions.

So, getting out of our comfort zone doesn't require a lot. We don't need fancy trips, expensive meals, weekends away or lots of fancy clothes. What we need is a catalyst, and being open to change and seeing things from a different point of view.

Working from home was only one of the comfort-zone leaps I had to make. There were many others, not least my glamming routine! I used to have my hair and makeup professionally done for all events or filming. Now, no matter how many ways I tried to find a solution, there was no way I could smuggle a full hair and makeup team in through the bathroom window, so I had to learn to do all that myself. I have to say, it's very liberating to know that you no longer need to depend on others and you *can* be self-sufficient. It was a little nerve-racking before my first @mrsrodial Instagram Live sessions – no makeup artist, no lighting, this could trend in all the wrong ways – but it was fine, and I was pretty proud of myself. The same goes for having facials and plumping treatments. I can now make use of my full Rodial skincare range and masks for a fraction of the price of a professional treatment. It's always good to be saving money! It's really good for me to get back in touch with using my products at a really basic level, finding what still works, what I might improve, what I had forgotten about all the products in the collection.

Getting out of your comfort zone also means being open to new ideas, and another unexpected change to my regular routine was in fitness. Being at home all the time suddenly highlighted to me that I had plateaued a bit with my regular routine. I had been doing the pump workouts with weights on an online fitness platform, but doing the same workout day after day without any live classes to mix it up with meant I was coasting a little bit. Then I happened to miss my regular online class and, scrolling around for something else, I stumbled on something called the 'Flex & Punch' workout, which is based around boxing. Me and boxing don't go well together. I've never been a great fan of watching men (or women) punching each other's faces – so it wasn't a form of workout I was particularly looking out for, but, on this day I said to myself, 'What the hell ... why don't you get on this class? It's free and you've already got your moisture-wicking, bamboo yoga-pants on. Just start it and if you don't like it, you can switch off the iPad and leave. No commitment ... easy.' So I started the class, laughing at myself slightly as I imagined myself as a female Rocky, 'Eye of the Tiger' playing on a loop in my head, but as I went through the moves, I really started to love it. It was a great workout and I was moving my body in a way it hadn't moved before. All the moves were inspired by boxing but it wasn't a sweaty, macho grunt-fest; it was a quick, light and really, really fun session! I was thrilled not just by the workout, but because I had found another way of getting out of my comfort zone and trying new things.

So looking back at my New Year's resolution, it's true, I may not have followed the plan and led the glamorous 'out of my comfort zone' life I had imagined, but I was *really* getting out of my comfort zone as well as trying new things and mastering new skills ... and that felt good!

Sometimes we blame other people or our circumstances for not being able to get out of our comfort zone and live our best life. It's easy to blame our unhappiness and complacency on other people, but you know the truth: it's you setting those limiting patterns. Only you can give yourself the kick up the backside required to find the way out; you can't depend on others to do it for you. Let's say that your usual pattern is to work all day and then, when work is over you head home and watch TV. Then one evening your friends invite you to come out and join them for dinner but you can't be bothered (it's cold and dark and you are tired from work). You decide to stay at home as usual, comforted by the familiar groove you are in as you settle down for another night with Netflix. The day will come when you realise you don't love your life and you are not having fun. You blame your partner for not creating exciting plans when actually it's you that is stuck in that comfortable rut. You are the problem and, if you don't shake up that routine, you'll just get stuck even deeper. No one else will shake it up for you.

I want to take a minute to talk about routines. Routines help us get the mundane and simple day-to-day things out of the way so that we can focus our brain power on tackling more difficult challenges and being creative. I have developed a strong morning routine where I wake up at 5.30am every day so I can fit in a couple of hours setting my intentions, researching and working out to get in a positive headspace for the day ahead. My morning routine also includes having pretty much the same breakfast every day (greens and a protein smoothie) and also sticking to the same lunch and dinner menu, or at least variations of the same thing. I also take a leaf out of the Albert Einstein/ Steve Jobs book when it comes to my outfits for the office. They – and many other great thinkers – would have a wardrobe full of the same outfit, one set for each day. That way they didn't waste any brain power choosing what to wear and thus could get on with inventing iPods, devising the theory of relativity and generally being incredible thinkers. OK, so neither of them was particularly noted for being a style icon. I mean, they both had 'a style', but I am not one for stonewash jeans and a baggy black turtleneck, or elbow patches and a pipe. Instead, I have a few options in my closet but I still hold to the principle: I keep it small and I keep it simple. Outfit A, B or C. That's it. Suit up and then: Bam! Let's change the world!

It's the same with all of these routines and set situations. Following them without having to really think means I can focus on being productive and creative and deal with whatever challenge might be thrown at me in the day. However, as I have shown, routines can also be dangerous, and I became so rigid about them that I forgot to live life. Many was the time I'd be at an event, having a great time, when I would suddenly drag myself out of it to go home early because I 'had' to wake up at 5.30 in the morning. Sometimes the event had hardly even got going ... I saw a lot of 'welcome' drinks receptions and not many actual events. And then in the morning, having ducked out for an early night, I'd wake up with the lark full of inspiration to write a chapter for my book, but no, that's not in my routine ... first, I need to mediate, work out, listen to an inspirational podcast, etc., etc. So, by the time I'd ticked off all of my rigid schedule items, my inspiration to write that chapter had gone and I'd end up not writing it.

It got ridiculous sometimes, like the time I was hosting an overnight press trip and instead of staying overnight with my guests and enjoying the experience, I got a car back home so I could wake up early and not miss out on my scheduled gym session the next day. While my trainer would applaud this level of commitment to a workout, it wasn't doing me any good. I just wasn't enjoying myself. Now, I get it that sometimes it's good to have a 'Get Out of Jail Free' card in your back pocket to bail from an event if you need to ... in fact it's a joy sometimes ... but every time? Including the times you really would rather have stayed? That's tipping the scale too far. What I am trying to show you here is that while routines are good, and you should have them to organise your day, you need to allow some diversions, you need to be able to change your path and shake up the routine at times, to open yourself up to new opportunities and directions. The responsibility for enjoying your life falls to you.

Things that sometimes serve us for a long time and are even really positive, like routines and patterns, can become a bit imprisoning as they no longer fit us. We are constantly evolving. Our moods, attitudes, likes and dislikes are always shifting, and so the patterns we built around us seven years ago may not be the ones that fit with us now. Incidentally, the body's cells largely replace themselves every seven to ten years, meaning you are pretty much 'renewed' several times in your adult life. Whether this changes your likes, dislikes or appreciation of kale smoothies is up for debate but some people notice that skin complaints, allergies and the like come and go in seven-year cycles ... so it's not the pollen, it's you. All the more reason to change things up. Routines are good, but change is good too.

We may need to drop something from our normal routine in order to create space in our lives, which can bring freedom and creativity. This is something we are taught to avoid. We all are taught to fill our calendars, stay busy, keep things moving, keep things rolling. But when we create space, we also create the energy to welcome in new information. It's a growing worry that children whose lives are micromanaged by 'helicopter parents' shuttling them from piano lesson to dance class, from football practice to play-date, are losing the ability to play creatively. They need to get bored enough to explore the wonders of a stick ... it's a sword, it's a magic wand, it's a snake, it's a unicorn horn, etc., etc. The days when children were kicked out of the door in the morning to roam free all day and only came home for dinner are long gone, but people are starting to see that unstructured freedom is a valuable part of a child's development. For children, play is a natural instinct and allows them to examine the world and their potential by trial and error. Not allowing them freedom can inhibit this development and leave them less independent, less confident about their choices and capability. I believe it's exactly the same for you. Creating space for yourself is one of the most productive things we can do in order to welcome in positive action and positive connections, as well as new ideas and new creative inspiration. Are you keeping yourself locked up? Are you over-parenting yourself? It's time to reassess.

You may have been doing the same thing day after day, week after week, month after month, and eventually you just feel flat. Everything around us moves so quickly that what we did a year ago, even six months ago, doesn't cut it any more. The rules change all the time. You may feel you've been left behind, and when you look around you start to feel that everything and everyone is moving faster than you, everyone is ahead of the game.

So how can you make a change? How do you open up? Nothing exciting will come from just accepting the status quo. First of all, really look at the detail. It is about making micro-adjustments, not just assessing the big picture of where we want to be. We can start by looking at where our energy is going. Are you getting involved in things at work or in your personal life that just don't give anything back, or take more than you give? Things that don't give you a return can wear you out and feel heavy. If that extra work is feeling really empty and hollow, check where you are putting that energy.

It's up to us if we want to be open to whatever comes our way and tap into our intuition, particularly if we already lead busy lives. We need to be very discerning about where we spend energy. We have a tendency to hold tight to situations that aren't working for us any more, simply because 'we've got this far'. We need to reassess where we are putting our energy. Really look around yourself.

In short, to be open to new opportunities, new projects and new creative visions, you need to ditch some of your fixed routines and rituals in order to create moments of space wherever you can. This doesn't always have to start with huge revolutionary actions; it often starts with small, micro-adjustments, like considering what time you wake up in the morning, what time you go to bed, whether you are pulled into some weird little project that doesn't really serve you, or adding things to your plate that you actually don't need, literally and figuratively. Really question all the things you are doing and ask yourself, 'Why do I have to do this?' If it isn't helping you, consider dropping it. Don't be scared of the guilt culture. Let go of anything that's not serving you.

When we look back, we may feel we let ourselves down a bit by not realising this sooner or not taking risks or trying anything new. We may feel that we should have done something better or different or been more on the ball, but none of that matters. Don't worry about wasted time, it's gone. The time is now. So, it's OK to release, it's OK to let go of how we've acted in the past or, indeed, who we've been in the past. We can still show compassion to our old self, accept who we were and move in a new direction. It's like looking at a ridiculous haircut you had in college. You wouldn't want it now but, for whatever reason, you thought it was cool at the time … crimped backcombed mullet? Really? It's our choice to advocate for that visionary forward focus.

It's important to be clear about how you want to feel. Be clear, be focused. If it is something that you can't change immediately, figure out how you can make those micro-adjustments over time. The important thing is to be actively and proactively listening to what your inner voice is telling you. If that voice is telling you that you don't feel like you any more, then it's time to send out the search parties. Open yourself up to opportunities to connect with people and experiences that help you really own your destiny … and own it in a way that is extremely self-empowering. The starting point is to create space between you and the things and experiences that feel heavy. Give yourself permission to create a brand new you and, with that, a meaningful new future.

All you need is to make a decision *today*. A decision to take a step towards change. It could be a call, an email, a 'to do' list, just anything to take you in a new direction. Change is hard, I know, but don't make it harder by looking back and blaming yourself for things you didn't do right or were complacent about in the past ... coulda, woulda, shoulda. Leave all that behind.

Make that change and decide that *today* is a new day and a new you.

How to Live Your Best Life Secret #2

10 tips to get you out of your comfort zone

1. Find a new tribe. New people bring new energy. A tribe is not just the people around you, it can also be people that you follow on social media or people you read about or whose life you follow in the media.

2. Do one thing a day that will take you out of your comfort zone. It could be a small thing like trying a different online fitness workout going to a new coffee shop, making a stop somewhere inspiring and uplifting after work and before going home.

3. Take a different route to work. Instead of going right, go left. Discover a new way of getting to your destination; a simple but easy trick to get your mind thinking in different ways.

4. Try to get out of the office more and meet people that will bring value to your work.

5. Read a new magazine, pick up a new book, try some new food. Curiosity will get you out of your comfort zone and get you thinking in new ways.

6. Have a meeting with a colleague that you haven't spent that much time with yet and, if appropriate, find out how you can help each other achieve your goals.

7. Create a mood board of how you want to feel (it could be a physical or a Pinterest board). Include things that raise your vibe. Be as broad as possible.

8. Meditate for five minutes every day. This always helps create some space in your head for new ideas.
9. Book a trip for yourself. It could be a day trip or a weekend, just by yourself. And when you are on it, don't make any plans and go with the flow.
10. Challenge yourself daily. You will feel so much better about yourself. You will feel empowered and ready to take over the world.

3

Trust Your Instinct

April 2019. I get a call from a banker friend. He asks me to go for lunch to talk about investment for my business. It's lovely to hear from him but, letting him down as gently as I can, I remind him that I am not interested in getting external investment. Still, he insists that we meet for lunch. Hmm, I really don't want to, but I have recently promised myself to keep an open mind and entertain any new ideas, so off to lunch I go.

I have to say, this is not the first time I have been approached to sell part of my company, so my initial reluctance wasn't entirely based on routine; there is some hard experience in there. If you have read my first book, *How to Be an Overnight Success*, you will know that when I started my business, I tried to get external investment but failed to do so. Undeterred, I decided to launch Rodial from the back room at home with my £20,000 savings and, for the first few years, was living hand to mouth and packing products on the kitchen table. Since then, things have picked up a little and all the bankers, venture capitalists and bigger companies who initially marked me out to fail have reappeared, asking if I'm open to selling a piece of my business success. I can't lie, after the heartbreak and humiliation I felt when I was turned down, I do now enjoy the satisfaction of seeing them coming back to beg. But then, that's every entrepreneur's dream, right? Work hard, grow the business and then sell it for a big chunk of money, enough to retire somewhere exotic and never have to work again.

But then, I don't think like every other entrepreneur. I always said that as long as I was still happy to go to the office, run my business and get excited by what I do, I wouldn't get external investment. I have always felt that getting an investor is the first step to losing control. I used to work in banking, so I know the pattern. When investors come into a business, their plan is usually to grow it as quickly as possible and then sell it again a few years later to another investor, making off with a quick profit. So their agenda is very specific and doesn't really fit with the one that I have, which is to grow the business, use my instinct to make decisions, take risks and be my own boss.

However, after many years of doing this, I can't lie, there are moments when I do want to give up and go off to that island in the sun. As the business gets bigger, things get more complicated, there is more and more delegation, there are more and more decisions, more challenges and just, well, more! The last few months in particular had been extremely challenging as we were planning 60 new product launches over three months … 60! As you can imagine, there were a lot of moving parts. I won't bore you with details of the hours and hours of meetings and planning and mountains we had to climb to get the products ready to go. Suffice to say that there was a lot of pressure, not only to ensure the products would be commercial successes, but also to finance them, to find the money to get them into production in the first place.

This was where my head was when I agreed to lunch with the banker. Was the stress of running a fast-growing company making me drop my defences, or was it time to make a change? I turned up at the restaurant and we ordered. He is a friend, he knows me and I think he could see that I was stressed. After the small talk, he said to me, 'Maybe the time has come to let off some steam, release some control of the business and simplify your life.'

At any other time, I would not have remotely entertained the thought of selling part of my business or getting into bed with an investor but, under the circumstances, the idea suddenly sounded really appealing and I must have looked interested. He knew how I felt about this topic – we had talked about it in the past – so I imagine that he took the fact that I didn't throw my drink in his face for daring to ask me to sell my company as tacit interest. He took a deep breath and continued, 'What if . . .' he said, 'what if you sold a piece of NIP+FAB, got an investor to run it for you and you can focus on Rodial?'

Woah. Hold on. That sounded perfect. I would still keep full control of the business I started and I would get some support on our millennial brand (NIP+FAB), which had a huge growth potential. I suddenly had a vision of myself freed from the worry of managing two brands ... with so much space and time to think, creativity would be fizzing out of me. I guess I really have been working too hard, but yes, I could take my hand off the tiller a little, free my mind. And I definitely like the idea of 'letting off some steam'.

So, me being me, things moved fast after that. The first thing we did was put together a project team with a small circle of people at the company to prepare what is called an 'Information Memorandum' or IM. This is a detailed document showing past sales and future projections, as well as all the info on marketing, product and business strategy. I thought this was going to take a few days' work, maybe a week. I was wrong. To produce an IM to the level that was needed, my team and I had to work evenings and weekends for months to pull together the excruciating level of detail required. In the end, it took us five months to complete this gargantuan document and then we hit the summer. By the time we were ready to market the company to potential investors it was already August and all the big guys were holidaying in Sardinia (it's where they go now; it'll be somewhere else next year, then somewhere else the year after that. I've gone past trying to understand it but it's like a herd instinct).

When they finally got back and my bankers started connecting with them, we started getting all sorts of responses. The response you get from these guys doesn't just have to do with whether your business is good or not but whether it is the right size, right location and whether this is the right timing for the investors. Obviously, some of the first companies we contacted were ones who had been in touch with us before, in some cases begging us for a meeting. It was going to be sweet fighting them off as they threw larger and larger bundles of cash at me in a desperate bid to own just a tiny piece of my success. Maybe I could ask them to take part in some kind of gladiatorial challenge, while I luxuriate like a modern-day Cleopatra in a Dragon's Blood face mask and raise my thumb to the victor. As usual, in my vision I had slightly over-anticipated the reality. Far from fighting over the prize, not a single one of the investors was interested. The company is too small, too big, too UK-focused, not the right timing, too mass, too premium, too millennial, not mature enough, too hip, not hip enough, I don't like the packaging, we love the packaging but don't like the name. Argh!

If you have any self-doubt about your business, don't go on a journey to get an investment. It's the fastest way to self-doubt and second-guessing. Still, it wasn't all doom and gloom. In the end we had two parties interested, and after three months of calls, meetings, presentations, excruciating questioning and sleepless nights, we finally got an offer. But hold your horses and keep the cork in the bottle because the terms were nowhere near what we originally thought they would be. That wasn't all. The most concerning aspect was that the restrictions they were asking for could be detrimental to the rest of the Rodial business. This was a real trial. For three whole months, every day I came into the office with a black cloud over me. I had no idea when the project might come crashing down; one day the deal was on, the next it was off. It was a roller coaster … and riding along with me, of course, were my team. As well as everything else, I have to keep them together, and obviously they want to know where we are at. Are we getting investment, are we not? As a leader, I want to lead but I didn't even know where we were going, so what could I even say?

In the meantime, inevitably, I had dropped the ball on running the business. There is only so much you can take and so, one morning, instead of my stomach being tied in knots over the state of the business, I found that I awoke with a sense of clarity. All those years of following my instinct had led me to great success, and one thing it had consistently told me was that getting an investor wasn't the right thing to do. In a moment of weakness and exasperation I had gone against my instinct and look what happened. I had wasted time and energy on a project that was going nowhere and my business that I took years to build was going down the drain. If you read the introduction of my second book, *How to Make It Happen*, it describes what I went through while working on that deal; I took my foot off the pedal, lost control of the spend and expenses, and almost went bankrupt.

I had to follow my gut feeling now, which told me it wasn't working. Getting the investment at that point in time and with those terms just didn't feel right. And so, I shut the investment process down, decided to cut my losses and get my business back on track. On reflection, when I made the decision to get investment it was the right decision, I was ready. If the process had gone more smoothly, if the responses had been what we were looking for, I probably wouldn't be changing course now ... instead, I'd be bikini shopping and starting a subscription to *Retirement Island Monthly*. But you never know where things will take you. So, don't be rigid, follow your instincts but don't force it. Flow with it.

My instinct has served me well over the years. Most of the time, when I trusted it, I was right. When everyone was questioning if I had the skills to start my own business, I followed my gut and started Rodial. When people thought I was crazy by naming a product Snake Serum, I went with my instinct and launched the hero product that put Rodial on the map. Call it instinct, gut feeling ... you could even say it's 'the universe'. Maybe it is a power beyond logic that leads us to make the right decisions?

I've been thrown all types of challenges over the years and dealt with them one way or another. It hasn't always been easy and when I was in the middle of the storm I experienced all sorts of feelings and emotions: unsettled, insecure, weak, in pain, wondering if there was ever going to be a light at the end of the tunnel, and if there was, hoping that it wasn't an oncoming train. I faced situations that were dragging on for so long and put such enormous pressure on me mentally, I didn't know if I would ever get to the other side, but I kept going. No big plans. No trying to cover all possible eventualities. Just dealing with it one day at a time.

What I learned is that in our lives we never ever get sent anything we can't deal with. Looking back on the challenges

I had, I now saw these as a way to grow. As I mentioned earlier, 2019 had been a hell of a year and this wasn't the only time I had been overwhelmed, but I got through it and now I could look back and assess how I had survived. What I saw was that each of these near disasters had given me a way to connect more deeply with myself and develop new skills and behaviours. The only thing I needed to do was to show up and face the problem. It sometimes seems easier to avoid a situation by brushing it under the carpet – I have done that many times, too many to be honest – but the problem doesn't go away. If anything, it just gets bigger. So I had to learn to show up, stand tall and face it. I can't predict what I might face in the future, or know what you might be facing now, but don't think I'm being flippant by saying 'just face it'. I know it's hard, really hard, and I know it can be painful, but I also know that when I have faced up to a problem it has always put me on a journey of growth. A journey of self-awareness.

June 2017. We are about to shoot a campaign with a celebrity model for Rodial. Very exciting. This is going to be a real boost for the brand. We're a week away from the shoot, so things have been in motion for some time, but now they are in overdrive. The studio has been booked for months, we've had creative meetings with the photographer, countless sessions with the makeup and hair artists and everything is coming together. Just one small issue ... the contract with the model.

A game of contract tennis had been going on for weeks. Every amendment we proposed was coming back with a redline through it ... we just couldn't seem to meet in the middle. Now, this is the way it works with most bookings, so initially I wasn't concerned, but this was getting dangerously close to the wire, and there didn't seem to be anything we both agreed on. There was still so much to do for the shoot, and we were now at a standstill. Nothing else could be done until we'd got the ink on paper. We couldn't book the flight until we knew the model was coming, we couldn't book the car until we knew she was getting on that flight, etc., etc.

I read another chain of 50 emails between their lawyers and ours, and when my PR came to me with the twentieth problem of the day, I wondered why we were doing this. As I looked at the ticking clock and my stressed-out team and thought about the seeming intransigence of the agent, I just decided it wasn't going to work and I called it. Time of death: right now!

Mouths dropped open in the office. I felt a shiver of fear myself, I admit, but a weight had lifted. I was calm and serene. My PR went pale. We had paid a ton of money to hold the studios, book the photographer, design mock-ups, and now we were pulling the plug? As my PR asked if I was really, really, I mean, definitely, honestly, absolutely serious about cancelling, I explained that there were just too many obstacles, too many things working against this. It was a sign. If something is this difficult, we shouldn't do it and it's fine. After a beat, my PR then said, 'Er, you know, I don't think we can get any of our money back for the bookings.' We did try, but after a few calls my PR came back and in a very small voice told me what I sort of expected all along: we weren't going to get a refund. If you cancel within a month in this biz, you don't get your money back and we were a week away. I said it was fine ... and it was fine. I was positive and not stressed at all. Yes, we wanted to shoot the campaign. Yes, we were already committed to some elements financially, and my team had put so much into the project, but I knew I was cancelling it for the right reasons. It would have been great not to lose money obviously but, y'know, omelettes and eggs.

Another factor in this equation was that I already had a relationship with this celebrity model, and so I hadn't wanted to make her mad. When we called her agent to say we had shut the campaign down, they were understandably really upset. Not wanting her to think the decision was anything to do with her personally, I messaged the model directly and said I was really sorry it didn't work out, but we love you and we'd love to work with you again. Which was true. And she wrote something nice back to me too.

It was a situation that could have gone very differently, but we dealt with it in a calm, positive way, not overreacting or exaggerating every single detail or being annoyed, frustrated or disappointed. There were too many roadblocks, but don't worry about it, it's fine. It wasn't meant to be.

Instinct fuels your drive and work ethic. Instinct is really just passion disguised as an idea. When you work on ideas that you really care about, you are more likely to be right and more likely to work hard enough to succeed.

I learned a lot from this episode. There were two paths we could have chosen. We could choose to go ahead with a contract we didn't feel comfortable with, wasn't going to give us the results we needed and could potentially compromise our objectives. Or we could walk away from it, lose some time and money and maybe upset an agent … but the loss and the regret of that course could have been much higher in the long run. So, having weighed the options, I went with my gut feeling and let the universe guide me, and at that point the universe was telling me this is just not right: walk away. So I did.

When we go into a situation with loads of intensity and baggage we may not be creating the right atmosphere for things to happen. When we take a step back, cultivate a positive attitude and let the universe do its magic, great things can happen.

Go with the flow, not against it. Do what feels natural. Keep your cool and try to see the other person's point of view. Don't force any situations and follow your gut feeling. Protect your energy. Stop overthinking and overanalysing, and direct your energy into your goals and creativity. Results will come when you do things effortlessly. That's when miracles happen.

Align with your true self, with your highest power.

How to Live Your Best Life Secret #3

10 steps to help your instinct guide you

1. Follow your idea. When you can't get an idea out of your head, your gut is telling you it is worthwhile. If an idea keeps you awake at night and you can't stop thinking about it, it means that you have to deal with it one way or another. Don't ignore it.

2. Commit yourself to your idea. Your instinct needs to be supported by dedicated work. The faith that you have in your mission will keep you going and will help you overcome challenges more easily.

3. Immerse yourself in your idea. Get to know every little detail of your passion project. That knowledge of your industry or project will help you focus and make the right decisions.

4. Ignore the rules. The rules may be saying one thing, but your instinct may say something else. Just because the rules say XYZ or other people would choose to take the path from A to B, it doesn't mean that you have to do the same. Going with your instinct means you have faith in your idea, and you shouldn't be afraid to ignore the rules.

5. Be flexible. It may be that your instinct was telling you to go for it but then along the way situations change or challenges come up that seem to tell you otherwise. You need to be flexible to listen to your

instinct every step of the way and keep listening to it as the plan and the course of action change. What was right at the beginning of the project may not be right any more.

6. Be a good listener. When we are in the middle of a crisis, we may raise our walls and block out what is going on around us. Try to clear your head, listen properly and make a decision when you are calm, cool and collected. Let ideas marinate, take it all in, sleep on them before you take action.

7. Let bad feelings go. Research has shown that we make better intuitive choices if we are in a positive mood. If you are tired or in a bad mood, wait until you calm down and are in a better frame of mind to make the right decision.

8. Be conscious about the people who surround you. People who drain you will add to the noise and cloud your judgement, preventing you from making the right decision. Surround yourself with people who enrich and empower you. Positive people will let the power stay with you; those who are negative will be pulling the power over to them.

9. Be silent and still. Our intuition is always sending us messages, warnings and encouragement but, when we are busy, we don't take notice. Practise mindfulness, meditation and self-care to inject moments of stillness in your day.

10. Pay attention to your dreams. Dreams are a way of processing the information that's left over from the day. Paying attention to our dreams can give us detail that we may not have access to during the noise and bustle of our busy days. Before your sleep, think about a dilemma that you are going through, and about possible options and solutions to that dilemma, and let your mind do the rest.

4

Own Your Happiness

You are what you think. You become what you think. What you think becomes reality.

It doesn't matter where you are in business and in life, there are always situations that can cause drama, anxiety and unsettlement. You may be doing as well as you could ever think but there are always curveballs that drive you mad and can mess with your energy, peace and sanity.

You may be in your twenties, and just starting your career or your business, or in your thirties or forties and thinking, what is she talking about? If I had the career that she has, my life would be perfect.

Let me take you back in history for a moment.

Look, there is me at eight years old. I'm writing a list, obviously. On that list are all the things I want to achieve, all the things I want to be … I wrote a lot of those lists. Even at that age, I always had a very clear vision of who I wanted to be. I visualised being very successful, working in a glamorous industry, travelling all over the world, meeting fascinating people and having an interesting and exciting life. I had a very clear plan of how I would get there and, although that plan changed, I knew I'd need to work really hard with a steel focus to achieve my dreams. My eight-year-old self thought that achieving those goals and ticking all those boxes would bring me eternal happiness.

What my eight-year-old self didn't know is that success is not straightforward – it has a lots of ups and downs – and I couldn't bear to break the news to that sweet little eight-year-old girl that success doesn't always bring happiness. Even if it did, that happiness also has its ups and downs: nothing lasts forever, happiness is not a permanent state. Just as well too: how can you tell if you are happy if you have never been sad?

A lot of us fall into what is called the 'destination trap'. This is the idea that achieving the next goal, the next job, the next holiday, the next purchase, the next partner is going to fix us and make us eternally happy. The term 'destination addiction' was coined by British psychologist Dr Robert Holden to describe the trap that some of us fall into, believing that the future is where happiness or success lies, that somehow success is a destination, just ahead on the journey, but we never actually arrive ... and we are so busy rushing to get to this golden tomorrow, we never savour the moment or stop to smell the roses. We live in hot pursuit of some imagined bliss that is always just around the next bend. It's a real barrier to success.

If I look at my goals over the years, I have probably ticked every single box of what I wanted to achieve in my life, both personally and professionally. I've built a business I am very proud of, I have a family I love, I have written two books and made a name for myself. So, do I wake up every day feeling the happiest person on the planet? Is my life always perfect? No. There are always highs, and there are always lows. But even before the New Year revelation, when things were in perfect balance and I can definitely say I was happy, I had good days and bad days. There were good days when I felt inspired and everything seemed to be working perfectly: I'd come up with amazing product ideas, meet inspiring people, attend glamorous events and get great feedback on my work and all that was positive. All the cool stuff helps me deal with the days when I am facing down lawyers, accountants and disgruntled aunts.

That eight-year-old would be proud of me. I pretty much followed her plan and ticked off her lists. Looking back at my life journey and how I achieved all this success, I have come to realise now that a lot of the time I was operating in that destination addiction mode. I was putting on the armour and diving into battle, not worried about the toll it was taking or the injuries I was subject to. I was working on the assumption that life is all about achieving those goals and, once these are achieved, I would be eternally happy. Launching another successful product? Tick. Reaching millions in turnover? Tick. Poaching that sales manager from a competitive brand? Tick. Getting married and having kids? Tick. Buying that latest Bottega Veneta sold-out sandal? Tick. That was it. Happiness forever, right?

Of course, once I made those goals, I would become unsettled and needed another fix. Another successful product launch, another Bottega shoe, another business goal. That's normal, that's what makes a successful business person keep on climbing the mountain and all that. So, I would raise the bar, make some new goals, write some new lists and that would keep me running on the road to success. But of course, it wasn't a road, it was a treadmill. I might have been achieving great business success but I wasn't going anywhere in my life. I was always on a high chasing another goal and another material possession, trying to get to that point of ultimate happiness. Those moments of success and what I thought was happiness would quickly disappear and get me chasing the next moment of happiness. Essentially, I was just going from one fix to the next, but nothing lasted. Somehow I sustained this for all these years, and for a while it seemed to be working ... but then the battle turned. I had no more reserves, the tipping point tipped and here I was looking back and going, 'Oh, I get it now.'

I recently bumped into an old acquaintance of mine on one of my store visits to check out our Rodial counters. I hadn't seen her for a while, and she looked amazing! She'd always considered herself overweight and had obsessed for years about it. As we had coffee the subject came up. 'You know,' she said, 'I always thought that if only I could lose all this weight, I would be the happiest person on earth.' Not only had she reached her target weight but she has changed her look and style. She looked so glamorous, and she looked happy. I congratulated her on achieving her goal and told her how proud I was of her. She paused and smiled, and then she said to me, 'Maria, you know what? The reality is, I am not as happy as I thought I would be. Don't get me wrong, I am thrilled with my achievement. But I thought this was all I needed in my life to be happy. It wasn't.'

As with so many of us, she had fallen into the destination trap. The thought that once we achieve a certain goal, we will be happy forever. We've been conditioned to believe that there is somewhere better than the here and now that will lead to happiness.

'I'll be happy when I ... find the right job/meet a new partner/move to a new city/take that holiday/make more money/start the business/lose the weight.'

The problem with thinking that happiness is somewhere else is that you will never be happy with what you have. This doesn't mean we should all stop having goals and trying to achieve things in our life, but this needs to be balanced with accepting and being grateful for our current situation first. We all need to have a purpose in life and enjoy the journey of working for a certain goal and getting that sense of achievement. When we get there, we can afford a brief moment of high-fiving ourselves before coming up with a new goal and/or coming to terms with the fact that life has its ups and downs and that the newfound happiness is not going to be as long-lasting as we hoped.

We tend to attribute our happiness to something other than our thoughts. But our feelings can only come from inside us.

Conversely, we attribute a lack of happiness to external circumstances. We believe it's 'stuff' that is preventing us from being happy. We often say to ourselves: I am not successful because of my upbringing. I will be free once I quit my job. I will be secure when I have money in the bank. I'll be successful once I get that job. I'll be devastated if my partner leaves me. I have a fear of failure. I feel anxious about this meeting. I can hear myself here and I am sure you can hear yourself too. This is another way of relying on or blaming external factors for our happiness. We create feelings and situations by overthinking, and we are very good at convincing ourselves these feelings and situations are genuine. They are not, and they are not the key to our happiness or lack of it.

This reminds of an old joke. On his beat late one night, a police officer sees a man desperately searching for his keys under a lamppost, so he decides to help him. After half an hour of fruitless searching the police officer asks the man, 'Are you sure you dropped your keys here?' 'No,' says the man, 'I dropped them over there, but the light is better here.'

Each of us is looking under a lamppost for a key that isn't there because it's the easy option. This happens when we are looking outside for happiness. The same argument could be made for those of us seeking security, resilience, fulfilment or success.

It's time to ask yourself, are you living in the present or are you so deep in your thoughts that you are experiencing something very different to your current situation?

Thinking is something we just 'do', but you can train your mind to think in a different way. On average we have around 60,000 thoughts a day and of those around 99 per cent are repeated. We are going over the same things again and again. If we let them, our thoughts can soon consume us. We end up overthinking so much that our thoughts become our reality and that makes us suffer. Until we realise that the problem is not our current reality but the fictional reality that we create in our minds, we won't be able to do anything about it.

Two people watching the same movie can have two very different experiences based on their backgrounds, emotional state, issues on their mind and relatability (and whether they like superheroes or not). The movie is an immovable object, it can't change, but our reaction to it can.

Likewise, two people engaged in the same job can also have very different experiences. Worker one feels energised, inspired and motivated; worker two feels deflated, stressed and unhappy. Same job, but they are experiencing it in very different ways. It's kind of like an emotional version of Einstein's theory of relativity where time travels more slowly the deeper you are in the 'gravitational well' (or something like that), except in this case time travels more slowly the deeper you are in your own mind (or something like that).

What I am trying to say here is that our perception of reality is created by our own thoughts. We may be in the perfect place for happiness – fulfilling job, perfect partner, money and possessions in abundance, solid friends and a great life – but if in our mind we analyse and create a negative, stressful, sad story about ourselves, that is what we are going to experience ... and no amount of material triumphs will overcome it. We will experience the illusion of our thoughts, rather than our reality.

Of course, there are ways to overcome this state, and this can be where addictions start. To quieten overthinking, people may use alcohol/drugs/shopping/gambling as an 'intervention' that gives temporary relief to these thought patterns and the painful feelings that come with them. Attempts to medicate against these agitated feelings are not really fixing the source of the problem – they give only temporary respite. Once the high is gone, the old feelings return, except this time you've added addiction to your list of woes ... but the attraction of a quick way to forget your troubles is not hard to understand. In Irvine Welsh's *Trainspotting*, a character going cold turkey, facing up to a list of real-life troubles in his newly clean state, fondly thinks back to the time when his only thought was getting the next hit of heroin. Life seemed so much simpler then. But as we know, the 'hit' of happiness is fleeting, and chasing it ultimately brings a smaller and smaller sense of fulfilment ... and when it has passed, the emptiness remains.

Now, I am not saying overthinking is quite on a par with being a heroin addict, but each of us gets hypnotised by the same order of illusion. When we worry or daydream. When we stress out because of work or traffic. When we are excited about a meeting or a date. I am not saying 'stop thinking' – I am saying stop overthinking controlling your reality.

Another downside of overthinking is procrastination. It is amazing how many things you can find to do while you are avoiding starting the thing you are meant to be doing. My favourites are:

1. Handbag stock-take: you can spend hours emptying the contents of your handbag – items that have been in there since before the millennium emerge alongside the old tissues, long-forgotten makeup brushes, three packs of gum all with one piece in, broken charging cable, phone number that creepy guy gave you on the tube, heel plasters (new), heel plasters (used), leaky pen, out-of-date coupons and one or two actual useful items. Line them all up, throw away the tissues and then put the rest back in your bag.

2. Deep clean mode: it's incredible how, after living quite happily with the state of your desk/bathroom/ entire house for weeks, the moment you need to start a challenging project you simply *have* to clean up right now … and I mean really clean up. Cupboards are emptied, scrubbing brushes are deployed, rubber gloves are engaged. We are talking toothbrush detailing here, folks. Once the hair goes up in that ponytail there is no turning back.

3. This is the equivalent of arranging deckchairs on the *Titanic* … otherwise known as the joy of pointless rearranging. Men like to alphabetise their record collection; I like to rearrange my closets. Shoes in colour-coordinated rows. Bags by colour or by size? Should long dresses be at the left or right? I'll just try on all of these dresses now, etc., etc. Hours of deferment fun.

4. The internet … all of the internet. I shall say no more on this.

While doing some of these things is enormously satisfying, it is not what you set out to do. All of this procrastination is just another form of overthinking and is blocking you from making a start. You want to start a project, but you start thinking of all the obstacles that will come your way and put it off until the mythical moment when you are 'ready'. Even if you are not the sort of person who procrastinates by throwing yourself into aimless physical tasks, you can still block yourself with aimless mental activities. Fear of failure crops up. You think about that project six months down the line and convince yourself that the worst-case scenario will happen. You convince yourself you will fail before you even make a start and so you never get off the starting blocks. Your mind is full of ideas but you can't see the light. You've been overthinking.

Alongside procrastination is the idea that in order to be worth the effort, the result must be perfection, and while pursuing perfection is admirable, giving up before you start on the basis that you might never achieve it is just self-defeating in the extreme. You convince yourself that if things are not perfect, you won't be happy. The pursuit of perfection doesn't allow you to enjoy the moment. You always find something negative in every situation. This is often referred to as 'Goldilocks syndrome' – where everything should be not too hot, too cold, too soft or too hard but 'just right' and, if not, it is rejected. Instead of letting this fear stop you from getting started, use the energy you get from striving for perfection to push you to higher levels. As every artist knows, the happy accident in the act of creation often produces a greater work than they could ever have imagined in their narrow vision of 'perfect'.

I have an admission to make: I am a perfection chaser, but I have found ways to work with it. One of these is to project positive words so that we wire our minds to think positively and not try to find that one small detail that may not be 100 per cent right. Let's say that someone in my team has done a great job on something, I used to say, 'You've killed it!' Lately I have come to realise that is a negative word even though it's used to describe something positive ... the subliminal mind hears negativity. I now say, 'You've done an amazing job, I'm very proud of you,' and that sends positive vibes to both my team and back to myself. Another subtle change I have made is instead of saying, 'I can't wait to see you,' I say, 'I look forward to seeing you,' leaving out the word 'can't', which immediately sends negative connotations. It's not easy to do and I have to think and practise, but it's a great way to always keep focusing on the positive and sending out positive vibes even if everything isn't perfect.

Another 'overthink' it's easy to succumb to is the feeling that you somehow don't belong here. You may have achieved a lot but you still see your struggling self from years ago. You have reached a level of success but somehow think you are going to be 'found out'. You still see yourself as 'Jenny from the Block'; you can't see what you have achieved and how far you've come. Your limiting beliefs are holding you back. You blame being unhappy on your background and how you've been raised, and I'll cover this in more detail in a later chapter. I was raised in a remote island in Greece and on paper didn't have the education, money or connections to help me follow my dreams. I could have used those excuses to avoid doing anything with my life, but I decided that my background wasn't going to define who I was. I had a vision, I had dreams and I wanted to make something of myself. I had to make a determined effort to block all those limiting beliefs and think of myself as not defined or restricted by them. It was tough sometimes, as I walked on the red carpets and sat at the head table of boardrooms around the globe, but I did it. I walked like a boss ... so I was a boss. How you think of yourself defines who you will become.

How to Live Your Best Life Secret #4

10 tips on how to stop overthinking

If you have a habit of overthinking, you may be preventing yourself from living your best life. Overthinking, in the ways I have described in this chapter, almost always ends in a negative spin, and an overactive mind can make you anxious, stressed and unhappy. Changing these patterns is a challenge, but with practice you can train your brain to perceive things differently and reduce the stress of overthinking. Learning how to improve the way you approach life's challenges is one of the greatest gifts you can give yourself. These are ten tips to help you stop overthinking:

1. Identify the problem. Become aware when you start overthinking and identify the subject. Sometimes we don't even realise that we're doing it, so the first step is simply to identify what it is that we overthink about.
2. Write it down. Write your thoughts down in a journal every night or first thing in the morning, not necessarily in order. Do a 'brain dump' of everything in your mind.
3. Pay attention to your feelings. Say to yourself, I am feeling anxious and uncomfortable. Where am I? Am I in my head? Recognise that you are too much in your head rather than reality, and try to snap out

of it immediately. Distract yourself with something that requires focus. Interrupt your thought patterns as many times as you need during the day and this way you will train your brain to stop overthinking.

4. Look at the problem from a different time perspective. I find this one really effective. Ask yourself how important this issue is going to be in say, a month, a year, two years, five years and so on. If you can apply some time perspective to a problem, it won't look as massive as it does in your mind right now, which is a key tool in shutting down overthinking.

5. Take a step back and be in the moment. Meditation, working out and yoga are all excellent ways to calm your mind. Choose something that allows no room for other thoughts. A friend of mine used to enjoy rock climbing for this very reason, as she told me, 'When you might fall 50 foot off a sheer rock face at any moment there is very little time to worry about anything else ... the prospect of sudden, painful death tends to focus the mind.' Well, whatever works for you, I guess. Of course, another benefit to this was she was always outdoors. I believe that spending time in nature can be a great head-clearing, positive distraction; boosting your endorphins can help calm down your mind.

6. Make progress rather than wait for perfection. It's better to make an imperfect start and get a project going, rather than wait for the moment when everything is perfect. Overthinking can lead

to procrastination, so loosen up and don't expect everything to be just perfect. Just move forward any way you can.

7. Break old patterns: just because a situation hasn't worked out in the past it doesn't mean that it won't work out next time. You may be overthinking the problem and projecting old patterns and assumptions, leading to a negative outcome in your mind. Give it a fresh perspective and approach, and start again with a positive attitude.

8. Get your day off to a good start. Set the tone for your day and don't dive straight into the morning news, which is invariably depressing, stressful and negative ... full of politicians refusing to give a straight answer to a straight question. What is wrong with them? Just answer the goddam question! OK ... see what I mean? Just thinking about it set me off there. I'm not saying live in a bubble, but consuming stressful and negative information at the start of your day can set you off in a negative mood. Instead, start as you mean to go on by reading or listening to something uplifting, and set your controls to positive for the day ahead. This helps minimise overthinking and negative thoughts right from the get-go.

9. What's the worst that can happen? Always ask yourself that question in every situation that you are overthinking. Does anybody die? No? Then chances are that you can live with the worst-case

scenario, which even if the thing ends in a full-scale meltdown, probably won't be as bad as you imagine. Been there, bought the overpriced T-shirt. Realising and accepting the realities of any situation, both good and bad, can minimise the severity of your overthinking.

10. Connect with other people, especially people who don't tend to overthink. Ally yourself with people who are light and positive, whether around you or digitally. Lighten up.

5

Set Your Boundaries

Go where your energy is reciprocated, appreciated and celebrated.

Since I started my business, I have had to deal with all sorts of different people, including a few difficult ones, and dealing with difficult people is never a walk in the park. A lot of the time you get an immediate impression, the old social spider-sense begins to tingle as soon as you meet someone and you just know within seconds of the first air-kiss that you are not going to get on ... which is very useful for both of you as you can both then studiously avoid each other for the rest of the meeting/party/workday/your entire lives, and the universe remains in balance. It's a bit trickier if they somehow think you are destined to be BFFs and you are not so keen, but you soon learn how to work up your 'keep spotting someone on the other side of the room' or 'just need to take this call' social defences and save yourself from awkwardness and, crucially, being worn down. However, there has been the odd time where my radar has failed me spectacularly, notably in job interviews.

People have their best face on when they interview. They are in first date mode, smiling, easy-going, interested in you, all 'please' and 'thank you' and polite laughter ... you know what I mean, gold standard best behaviour. While with some people the varnish is easy to see through, with others the interview face is so convincing that they have slipped through my net. To be clear, I am neither claiming to be nor am I looking for Mother Teresa with a business degree and killer heels (although I do have both those things). I am just looking for people who click with me, click with the business and can bring the right skills and attitude to the job. Over the years my interview techniques have got better – and I can't believe how generally lucky I have been with the people who have worked with me as I grow my business, but no matter how rigorous the process it's never 100 per cent foolproof. I'm big enough to admit ... I got fooled. To be honest, you never really know anyone until they start and they have been on the job for at least a few weeks. You can get an idea from meeting them – talking through typical business scenarios and seeing how they respond, all the usual stuff – but it's only when they are on the clock that the real personality starts to show.

Early on in my business, things were starting to pick up and I was in the position of having to make some leaps to keep things growing. One of those leaps was hiring a marketing manager and so, after a long, and I thought, thorough interview process, I settled on someone who I thought was ideal for the job. However, while she was a whizz at marketing, she was also really hard to deal with when it came to everything else. She was one of those people who always saw a negative side to every single thing that happened. Being a generally optimistic, make-it-happen kind of person, I value the odd devil's advocate in the team, but this was more than just looking at it from both sides ... she was a doom-monger in Dior, bad news in Burberry. She was getting me down!

Apart from the general negativity, she seemed to always be building some kind of conspiracy theory that everyone was against her, at one point even claiming someone from the business was logging into her email and reading all her communications. Suffice to say, she was a hard person to deal with but, more importantly, her attitude was affecting the way I worked. Instead of springing out of bed with new business zeal each morning, I awoke with a sense of dread, wondering what new drama I was going to have to face with her today. If she had been dealing in hard truths about the business I could have handled that (I love a good meeting room debate), but her attitude had nothing to do with the business and everything to do with the way she was as a person ... and her paranoia kept us all on the back foot. We never knew what was next, and most of the time had no idea what she was paranoid about. She seemed to lash out at the tiniest and most inconsequential things, making random accusations and demanding attention at every turn.

At first I thought, 'Oh it's a one-off, she'll settle in.' While noting the exchanges between her and others, I let it go but, as I discovered, this was the real person, and the 'interview' person had been someone different. I had to step up and 'be the boss'. My initial reaction was to lash back and cut this attitude dead, and I did that a couple of times but it didn't feel good. I've never been one to shout and stomp my foot, but I figured that this might be the only thing she would respond to, so I would adopt my power stance, take a deep breath and deliver a wall-shaking big-boss rant. The entire office would fall silent, the clicking of keyboards would stop and everybody would freeze while I tried to fight fire with fire ... but, in the end, it was me who got burned. Each time I did this, I would turn on my heel and close my office door with a flourish only to dissolve into a quivering wreck seconds later.

This way of dealing with people was not me, and the toxicity of these exchanges was landing back on my head and having more effect on me than on the intended recipient. So I decided to change my attitude and, instead of lashing back, I would try to make her feel more positive and feel good about herself. The next time she lashed out at me, I didn't lash back. I coolly addressed the facts. If she said this person did this and that person did that, instead of diving deeper into the who did what and when, which in the past had ended up with her dragging me down a rabbit hole, I would ask, 'So, for you to be successful at your job, how can I help?' I moved the conversation away from toxic gossip and drama and into facts, action and solutions. I was trying to be the bigger person and by not reacting and hitting back at the toxicity, we found a middle ground, which in the end helped us to have a good relationship. I was responding and handling things in my way instead of being dragged around on her roller coaster. This way I felt I protected myself and, by hitting back with positivity, I managed to not only feel good at the end of every conversation but, in the end, we coexisted a lot easier ... and both I and the business benefitted from that.

Did my relentless positivity change her into a different person? The answer is probably not, but that isn't the important part of this story. The lesson I learned was that although it was early on in my business and although I did deal with it in the best possible way I could, I now realise that I should have dealt with the whole situation much earlier and set boundaries. If I had set boundaries early on, we wouldn't have ended up where we did. Boundaries are key to any relationship in life.

I use my @mrsrodial account on Instagram a lot. Yes, sure, there are a lot of pictures of my shoes on there and quite a sizeable proportion of me with various bags, but I use it mainly to communicate and do research. I did a poll recently and asked my followers to name what drains their energy. I had the marketing-manager saga in my mind when I asked the question but I wasn't sure how others would respond. One thing I did know, however, was how important it is to identify what drains our energy. It is only by identifying the thing (or things) dragging us down that we can develop strategies to be the master of our own energy, and to be unaffected by any negativity or general 'bad juju' that swirls around us every day. Put simply, by managing our own energy, we manage our own happiness.

When the answers started coming in, it seemed the thing that most identified as their big energy drain was other people. There were stories about toxic, difficult people, people who moan about problems they could probably fix themselves, people who complain constantly about minor things, people who play the victim, people who depend on us as though our own dreams don't matter, people who all see the negative side of everything (the type that always have a 'but what if ...' response), people who don't accept us, people we don't align with but just can't escape from, like work colleagues or housemates, people that hide behind a job or position and make our jobs harder, fake people and people that just bring us down! Then there were other responses that reflected on the effect on themselves: the people whose energies were depleted from constantly putting others first and neglecting their own self-care, jealousy from both sides, struggles with relating to certain people on a personal level, wasting time on ungrateful people, being held back by people who are scared to try or move forward, doing a good job and being underappreciated.

It's quite a list! Can you identify with any of these?

Of all the varied responses, one of the most recurrent answers was simply 'Toxic people'. Toxic people will come into your life in all kinds of different shapes and forms and will be a drain on your energy. If you can identify and avoid these people in your day-to-day life then that's great, or at the very least you can be ready for them in the few moments you do need to engage. However, I can guarantee that there will be some that you just cannot escape. They are likely to be family members, close work colleagues, friends of friends or (one that comes up a lot) partners of friends. When we spend time with them we feel our energy sapping out of us, we can't respond, we feel uncomfortable, we try and be witty and it comes out wrong, we don't feel confident, can't relax, we get clumsy … what are they doing to us? These toxic people are what we call energy vampires. They have such a powerful effect on us that whenever we spend time with them, we feel deflated, sad and unsure about ourselves. Avoiding them or gently taking a step back from that relationship is the best thing, but if that is not possible and we can't move away, we have to find strategies to protect our energy, be in control and not let them affect us. We need to set our boundaries.

Toxic people can be negative, always seeing the glass half empty, wanting to take us and our ideas down. This may stem from their own insecurities and a need to take others down to their level, but it can also come from a need to gain attention, quite often by playing the victim. They are usually excellent emotional manipulators and know exactly what they need to do to drag us into their orbit. It may be that we have been co-opted into their personal drama somehow, with us believing that we need them to survive or vice versa. Similarly it could be a co-dependent situation where we end up doing all the work to save them/ the situation while they behave like the victim, or it may not be as involved as all that. They could just be the sort that plays mind games, or just a loud, brash personality that needs constant centre-stage attention.

The first step is to identify the toxic person and/or relationship, and sometimes they can be hard to identify. They are so good with their mind games that you start questioning yourself and they can make you feel you are the source of all their problems ... and actually, they are not bad people, they are just bad for you. I have been writing about them as though they are a different species but they are not. You will find that someone who is toxic to you is perfectly fine with everybody else. Sometimes it's doubly hard to identify them as a toxic person because 'everybody *loves* Karen', and 'Hey, we are all going to Sally's tonight, you *must* come!' and 'Sally is *so* funny ... maybe you just don't "get" her?' Who could blame you for thinking the fault is with you? I'm here to tell you it's not. Sally and everybody else may be fine, but Sally and *you* is a toxic combination. It's like they are not toxic all the time, just under certain conditions or with certain people.

Recently I have found that this type of toxic person is most prevalent around those who are successful, positive, independent and quite often with some level of celebrity, and they try and drag you down, draining your energy to bring you down to their level. When they do that, they feel they have won. Needless to say, they can turn you into a mental wreck.

So, what can you do? You can't change other people, but you can change the way that you react to them. I would advise against trying to change them: the toxicity will just continue. You need to protect yourself first and look at it from an objective point of view. Take a step back, calm down and don't get drawn into the drama. If you must get into an argument, get into it in a Zen way. As Quentin Tarantino wrote in *Pulp Fiction*, 'Be cool, Honey Bunny!'

So toxic people are one thing, but what if your loved ones do not support you? That can be equally damaging to your energy and your drive. I fought many battles, but I am pleased to say I always had my family's support, even when sometimes I could tell they were biting their lip. Not long ago I was giving a talk at an event as part of London Fashion Weekend. This is a weekend open to the public where, for a nominal fee, they get to view designer collections and attend special events and talks. It happens straight after the London Fashion Week Ready-to-Wear shows each season and is a great chance for the general public to experience a little of the fashion-week buzz once all the buyers and editors have moved on to Milan. When I finished my speech, a young girl came over wanting to ask me a question. She told me that she had spoken to her family about attending this event. It was something she really wanted to do, she had read up on it and had become really excited about the whole weekend. However, her family had discouraged her from going, telling her that it was just a waste of time and money … shouldn't she be doing more important things? She was young, but old enough to make her own choices so, as was evident by her attendance, she decided to go for it anyway. I was very happy to hear that she felt really good that she had: the talks, the special events and shows and just being there, doing something she wanted to do, all left her feeling inspired and motivated, exactly what she hoped for. So, her question for me was, how could she deal with her family in the future, as they don't see eye to eye on her chosen path? She has her own dreams and they don't support her.

I advised her to be strong. When I started my business, I had a lot of people not believe in me. It didn't feel good to be knocked back or be on the wrong end of a raised eyebrow, but I decided it wasn't up to me to change certain people's perception of me. I found it was easier to keep my dreams to myself and I stopped sharing my plans with them so enthusiastically. Instead, I turned to those people who were positive, who encouraged me, boosted my energy and buoyed up my hope. I told her all of this and advised her to just keep thinking about her big goal. You know what you are aiming for, and if your family can't support it don't let them in on your vision. Obviously, they will still be in your life, but while they are you don't need to share your all of dreams and goals with them. This can be difficult with some parents, I know, but you need to set that boundary to protect yourself, your energy and your dream.

However, you don't need to go it alone. Instead, find your tribe. Get alongside those people who will understand and support you, whether in person or as part of an online community. That can be the platform where you can share your dreams, thoughts and passions. Spend more time and energy with your tribe. Limit the time you spend talking about your goals with anyone who wouldn't support them. You might give a broad stroke of what you are up to – otherwise people may think you a bit closed and secretive – but you don't need to share the details if they are going to shut you down every time. Also, not everything you do needs to be approved by your family, despite what they might say. They have a different background, different visions and expectations for themselves, and they live their own life. You are different.

As I mentioned previously, you can't change people, but you can change the way you react to them. It's not about who wins, it's about being at peace with yourself and being in control of your actions and reactions. Throughout my journey to become more spiritual I have given up on winning arguments and I can honestly say I have never been more at peace with myself. Be the light and this may rub off on people around you. I say 'may' as it won't work on everyone … but it's worth a try. Do it for yourself and see how much freer it makes you feel.

Relationships are hard. Whether it's with a colleague, a boss, a boyfriend, an ex or a relative, relationships can make us unhappy, but only if we allow them to overcome us and take control of our sense of self and our feelings. I can guarantee that in any workplace, family or large group of friends there is always someone around us that bubbles with negative energy and leaves us feeling drained. As discussed, sometimes you just can't avoid them, but it helps to identify them early. You need to use your gut instinct, of course, but what are some of the most obvious signs?

Negative people talk but don't listen. They think the rules don't apply to them. They create a lot of drama and want to control every situation. They blame others and don't take responsibility for their actions. They don't apologise. They feel entitled and they don't consider others' needs or feelings. They don't support you pursuing your goal. They put you down. They manipulate you in order to get what they want. They don't respect your boundaries.

Can you relate to this? Are you starting to work out that there are some people in your life that fit this mould? And if you are, how are you acting around them? How is their behaviour affecting yours? Do you put other people first before your own self-care? Do you allow people to judge you and do you let them in easily? Are you always sucked into dramas? Do you always feel you need to explain yourself? Do you feel obliged to answer personal questions when it doesn't feel right? Do you stay longer than you feel comfortable so as not to disappoint? Do you minimise your own feelings? Do you feel bad about your limits? Do you worry about other people's opinions if you speak up?

If so, it's about time to set some boundaries. Whatever you are willing to put up with is exactly what you will get. That's where boundaries come in. It isn't easy to set them but, when we do, we take the control back and it's very empowering. Boundaries are a way for us to take care of ourselves and, in a non-aggressive way, get what we want. Naturally, we become less angry and resentful as our needs are met. Boundaries clarify our expectations so others know what to expect from us and how we would like to be treated. The best way to enjoy happy and healthy relationships is to set our boundaries.

In an ideal world, people will respect our boundaries. But as we know (see: this entire chapter) there are people that will resist our efforts, argue, manipulate, blame, ignore, threaten and try to break us down. So, if we can't control how other people will act, we can learn to set our own boundaries and take care of ourselves first.

Setting boundaries is an ongoing process and there isn't a quick fix. We can't force people to respect our boundaries, but we can control how we respond when they try to break them down. If others don't respect your boundaries and you just let it slide, you are abandoning your needs to please someone else and just accepting treatment that you don't deserve, behaviour that will ultimately bring you down. If someone repeatedly violates your boundaries, you have to ask yourself how long you are willing to accept such behaviour. There are those who accept this sort of disrespect for years, hoping the other person will change, only to look back and realise that they had no intention of changing or respecting boundaries. Expecting someone else to change is a waste of your energy and, to be fair, it isn't really your job ... your job is you! As the flight safety instructions point out: fit your own mask before helping others. You'll be no good to anyone otherwise.

Don't forget that you have choices. You don't have to be in a relationship with someone who criticises you at work, a friend who takes advantage of your kindness or a family member who belittles you, or in a romantic relationship with someone who gaslights you.

The important thing to know is that you are not trapped or powerless. I know that choosing to end a relationship is painful and difficult, but it can be done. For practical reasons it may not be the time to end that relationship this very minute, but you can start taking the steps to untangle yourself from the situation, which will make it easier when the final showdown comes. The important thing is that, if you find yourself in this position, you must free yourself from the person who hurts you. Sometimes, we're not ready to end a relationship even though we know deep inside that it's unhealthy. I know that this is a very sensitive topic and there may be many factors to consider, but you can make a start by identifying your choices and detaching from this person by limiting time spent with them, avoiding being alone together, practising self-care and generally looking after yourself. Choose the best option and trust your instincts.

I realise that not everyone's experience is going to be that dramatic. But, in general, if you want to protect the energy around you, you can still say no to external triggers. You may be having your hair done at the salon and the stylist, meaning no harm, may start a conversation with you and you may not want to get into that conversation. I am not saying that every hair stylist is toxic, far from it ... what I am saying is that you are not obliged to open yourself up to others if you don't feel like it. If you don't want to, just say that you'd rather not talk and have some quiet time.

Now, you may be wondering how you can get away with saying nothing and not be rude? It's hard but if your tone is compassionate and you explain it in a way that's not rude or hurtful, you'll be surprised how readily people will accept your boundaries. Quite often, I get asked something personal, perhaps the old classic about whether I am planning any holidays. If I don't want to engage, I simply say, 'Not for now but thanks for asking.' I say it with a smile, but it's the 'thanks for asking' that shuts down the conversation in a polite way. Or just be upfront and put the emphasis on them with 'I hope you don't mind if I close my eyes or stay quiet during this? I am going to use the time to chill and think about my homework/business plan/Oscar acceptance speech.' Again, you will find that they are usually pretty accommodating ... and maybe relish a break themselves. Just find what works for you but remember to always protect your boundaries. Setting our boundaries should take priority over being popular and it is crucial for our sanity.

How to Live Your Best Life Secret #5
10 steps for setting boundaries

It is vital that you set boundaries for your life and the people you allow in it. A lack of boundaries invites a lack of respect, so what can you do if someone doesn't respect your boundaries?

1. Identify your boundaries and be clear about your needs. Know these yourself before you communicate them to others.
2. Communicate your boundaries or expectations in a clear, calm and consistent manner. There's no need to over explain, blame or become defensive: just stick to the facts.
3. Accept that there are people who won't accept your boundaries regardless of what you do. It may be disappointing, but you will need to decide if you want to continue with this relationship or not. You can't change someone else's behaviour, but you can choose to take a step back from the relationship.
4. If your boundaries are not respected, take action.
5. Take a step back. Taking a step back is a shift away from trying to control people and situations. This doesn't mean you don't care about this person, it means that you are taking care of yourself and being realistic about what you can do in this

scenario. When we detach, we stop trying to change others in order to get the outcome that we want and instead remain true to ourselves.

6. You can detach from a narcissistic or toxic person by:

    a. physically leaving a dangerous or uncomfortable situation;

    b. responding in a different way. Instead of taking something personally, you can make a joke out of it. This changes the dynamic of the interaction;

    c. avoiding spending time with them;

    d. letting them make their own decisions and face the consequences of their choices;

    e. not giving advice if not asked;

    f. avoiding participating in arguments and taking a step back from an unproductive conversation.

7. Limit or eliminate all contact. Sometimes the only way to protect your energy from toxic people is by limiting or eliminating all contact with them. This isn't to manipulate or punish them, it's self-care for yourself.

8. If someone is hurting you emotionally or physically, you owe it to yourself to put some distance between you and this person. You don't have to have a relationship with a colleague, family member, partner or anyone who makes you feel bad about yourself. If it's someone you can't avoid and have to see at a family or other gathering, you can still be civil but keep a polite and formal distance.

Focus on talking to other people and if you have to engage in a one-to-one conversation with that person, keep it very top line, talk about something generic. Don't share anything about yourself so you don't let them in.

9. Find a new tribe. The people you choose to have around you should lift and support you, not leave you feeling confused, angry, anxious or depressed.

10. Have a regular five-minute meditation practice. There are a lot of different meditations that you can find on YouTube that focus on gratitude and acceptance. They encourage you to focus on the things you are grateful for in life as well as accepting a current situation. It can help in taking away or calming powerful emotions so you can feel more Zen about it. Talking things out with a therapist can also really help.

6

Surrender
Your
Obsessions

When did admitting to having an obsession become OK? I'm pretty sure it used to be a bad thing ... just one step away from an addiction. The word 'obsession' has somehow become watered down and devalued. I blame Calvin Klein.

These days it's rare I open a magazine without it containing at least one article on 'My latest food/fitness/podcast/wild-swimming obsession' – and those Buzzfeed-type listicles would be a lot sparser without the endless posts on 'Ten eighties movies we're OBSESSED with!' Indeed, it sometimes feels that unless you have a conveyer belt of geeky yet stylishly on-trend obsessions to display and talk about loudly in company, you are somehow less interesting, less creative, less original ... less alive. I'm one to talk, as I regularly post pictures of my shoes, bags, etc. with #OBSESSED on my @mrsrodial feed. But although obsessions are now seen as generally unthreatening, fun, geeky things to have, a real obsession can be dangerous and negative. Imagine if a new partner said, 'I'm becoming a little bit obsessed with you.' You'd laugh, maybe blush, you'd think, 'Hmm, maybe a bit OTT, but nothing to worry about ... I'm actually a little flattered' – but there's a difference between someone who DMs you a bit too often and someone who has an apartment full of drawings, locks of hair, secret photos, toilet-roll sculptures and body-fluid paintings of you.

One is cute, the other is cause for concern. It's the second (and original) definition of 'obsession', the one where it starts to take over a bit too much, I wish to discuss here and show how, while it doesn't have to be quite at stalker levels, it can get in the way of you living your best life.

As human beings in a modern, civilised society, we have everything we need to be happy. I assume that you have bought this book with your disposable income or you were given it by a loving friend … or you have somehow the wit, verve and survival chops to have stolen it. Basically, you are doing OK. We are not scavenging for berries and hiding from sabre-tooth tigers any more; it's more likely we are looking for the perfect take-out coffee and hiding skin blemishes. But, when it comes to happiness, there is always room for more.

When we are actually happy and complete (great coffee, perfect skin, ripe berries, no sabre-tooth tigers, etc.), the room for more can be left as is. More good stuff may come to us, but we don't attach to it or obsess about it to the extent of having to go out and find it. On the other hand, when we perceive ourselves as unhappy or we are going through a low phase in our life, that is the time that obsessions typically start. These are the times when we are actively looking for something to give us happiness and when we are most likely to attach ourselves to some object of our desire, thinking it is going to fix everything. And you know what, it does work: having something to focus on, chasing that obsession, is initially soothing. It certainly is pretty good at distracting us from everything bad that is happening in our lives right now. At least you are doing something … right? Activity is surely better than inactivity? But having a goal is different from having an obsession. Having a goal is maybe getting a tattoo one day, having an obsession is a full body ink.

Meanwhile, life goes on as normal but we are not listening to it, we have a splinter in our mind's eye. The result is we abandon ourselves and we hand ourselves over to our obsession.

October 2019. We were gearing up for an exciting new product launch at Rodial: the CBD Sleep Drops. CBD (an abbreviation of cannabidiol) is the hot ingredient right now, and with the relaxation of laws and legalisation of cannabis products, particularly for health applications, ongoing around the world, we felt the time was right for us to market our own unique product using this wonder ingredient. Its use for pain management and controlling some forms of epilepsy is well documented, but it also has strong and proven skincare benefits, including calming skin irritation and reducing inflammation as well as stimulating receptors in our endocannabinoid systems. CB1 receptors channel the benefits of CBD to the brain and nervous systems, and CB2 receptors absorb the goodness into the skin and other organs. The research we put in to making this a premium and hopefully bestselling product was huge. CBD has for many years been perceived as a bit 'Sandals & Granola' – not really the Rodial demographic ... we wanted this to be the Gucci of CBD products!

This was a hot new launch for the business, so Gucci product = Gucci launch! We wanted to make as much noise as we could. The team and I planned to promote it with a series of events around the world. The events had to reflect the values of the Rodial Brand so had to be both luxurious and cool. We finally came up with the ultimate series of launch events. First would be a press staycation and dinner at the Nobu Hotel in London, then across the pond for a pamper day for the press at a healing spa in NY's trendy East Village and, to top it all off, a press and influencer brunch in a brand-new cannabis café in LA. It doesn't get cooler than that.

The London and NY events were important, for sure, but we planned the finale event in LA to be the largest, most exposed of the three. It was going to be a big deal. We hired the top events company in LA to source the location, organise the event and curate the guest list. We like working with the best and we were in great hands.

Our production company talked us through all the aspects of the launch, and we were especially excited to hear about the proposed venue ... the new and very hip cannabis coffee shop (only in LA!) where the theme of our CBD Sleep Drops would fit right in with the cannabis-infused soft drinks and cakes. In the weeks leading to the event our office in London buzzed with excitement and activity, updates and plans from the events company were pored over, we checked and double-checked the guestlist, confirmed RSVPs, approved table decor, haggled over what should be in the goodie bag, agonised over the wording of invites ... all the usual pre-production event stuff. This was going to be one to remember. As is the way with these things, the time shrank alarmingly as we neared 'CBD-Day' until, before we could say 'non-psychoactive extract', my team and I were on a plane and hurtling westwards from a chilly, rain-soaked (and typical) October day in London to the palm-fringed glamour of Los Angeles, California.

We arrived in LA full of excitement for the launch and, when we met for breakfast, we were warmed by a perfect LA morning. The sun was making its way across a clear blue sky, burning off the early morning mist in the Hollywood Hills, and the heat had begun to shimmer across the city streets. It was a blessed relief from the grey drizzle of England and the perfect setting for our launch. The brunch was planned at 12 noon and, checking through the final guest confirmations, we were thrilled to learn that the crème de la crème of the LA influencer, VIP and press community would be attending.

My team and I arrived at 11.45am to familiarise ourselves with the space before the guest started arriving, and ensure everything was as discussed, from the table decor to the goodie bags. The space looked amazing, a beautiful outdoor terrace with guest tables and food laid out, and a central presentation table where I would make a short speech and officially launch the product. There was just one problem ... as midday approached things were heating up. It was turning into a very warm day in LA. Even though it was October, the temperature was now around 38°C!

Hmm, that is quite hot, and that sun is getting quite intense. The terrace is going to be brutal. No problem, we just need to bring some shades out to cover the tables.

I collared a staff member. 'Oh, can you put a shade up? Or just a couple of large umbrellas would do it, thanks.' The pause between question and answer yawned like a gaping chasm. The waiter's eyes widened and darted around from café, to terrace, to blazing sun and finally back to me. 'Oh ... I am afraid we don't ... um ... we don't have any, like, umbrellas, or ... um ... shades.' He nervously gripped his tray and scurried back to the kitchen. I stood, gently venting steam as the implications of this hit me. Turns out that as the coffee shop had only just opened, they had not had a summer season before and so, like us expecting a temperately pleasant October in LA, had not actually got around to buying any sunshades for the terrace yet!

Small explosions were going off in my brain. Is there a store we can send somebody to buy some? Yes, but it's an hour away and guests will be here in five minutes. OK, can we move indoors? No, no room, every table booked for lunch. Can we redirect the aircon to the terrace? No. Can we blow up the sun? Apparently not.

Now, I'm not daft, I've been to LA before – I know it can be warm – but 38 degrees in October? The average temperature in LA for October is 26 degrees! I know this because as I stood there melting in the blazing sun, not quite believing this was happening, I whipped out my phone and googled it. Here is what I got back (the brackets are my reactions at the time):

> *Google Search: Weather in October for LA –*
> *Results: 'October is mild and pleasantly warm …'*
> (Pleasant? This is not pleasant … things are sticking to me where they shouldn't be sticking!)
> *'… with the average temperatures ranging from 58°F (14.4°C) to 78°F (25.6°C) …'* (Then what's with this 100°F, 38°C crap?!)
> *'Sunny days abound …'* (No shit Sherlock!)
> *'… with more than eight hours of daily sunshine, and the atmosphere is beautiful.'* (THIS IS NOT BEAUTIFUL … THIS IS A DISASTER!)

Air-conditioned limos and Ubers began lining up politely at the entrance, and from each one stepped a shimmering LA VIP. Outfits perfect, make-up perfect, hair perfect, mood perfect. Approximate time that look would remain perfect in a 38-degree solar furnace? About 30 seconds by my reckoning.

OK, so there is *nothing* we can do. I am losing it. My team rallies around, 'Let's just try and power through. Maybe it will be OK?' 'Make it happen, right?' They really are brilliant. Yes, let's get on with it. Maybe everyone will enjoy a nice sunny outing? Food is starting to circulate and it only takes the guests a few minutes to realise the central table doesn't have any shade, so they take their food and go and eat it in a corner.

The plan I had in my mind, the plan we had spent weeks discussing, the plan that was now being burned to cinders by the unrelenting West Coast sun, was for everyone to be gathered round the table, where I would give a short, informative and sparklingly witty speech introducing the product. Everyone would go 'ooh' and 'ahh', laugh and applaud before I was hailed as a saviour of skincare and the event would break Instagram and Twitter and all of the internet. None of this now looked likely.

So, with all this going on, what did I do? Well, dear reader, I admit I did the wrong thing. Instead of focusing on how this situation could be saved, I spent the whole time from guest arrivals onwards obsessing about what my vision had been and whose fault it was that this was all going pear-shaped. How had the events company got this so wrong? Why weren't the café staff doing more to help? How much money had I wasted on this? Why was this becoming the biggest disaster in the universe? Believe me, when you have a small business, it's hard not to fall into this trap. Every penny counts and, in my mind, we had just thrown a whole bunch of cash down the drain.

Meanwhile, while I was obsessing on getting answers *now* about what had gone wrong and who was to blame, the event was still happening, the guests we had worked so hard to get there were still sipping blood orange and cardamon CBD cocktails, and nibbling the amazing-looking chicken keto nachos. I may as well have not been there. I was so busy spinning around in my circle of 'it's all gone wrong' obsession that I barely said hello to any of the guests, let alone spoke to them about the new product ... the reason we were all there! Even when people made a beeline to talk to me I was disengaged, distracted and frankly a bit rubbish. I was mentally drained and physically frazzled. I was a mess. What a waste of time, resources and energy. Yes, it was a faulty planning issue, but then I just doubled-down and put the tin hat on the disaster by obsessing over the problems that were stopping this event being 'the perfection' I had seen in my mind's eye. If you are reading this, and you were there as my guest, I am sorry!

What should I have done? I could have taken guests inside, just a few at a time, sat by the bar, engaged with them, told them how happy I was they had come and done a quick two-minute informal version of the product spiel. It would have made the event personal; the product would have had its moment in the sun (ha!) and everyone would have been happy. Instead, I looked stressed, miserable and in no mood to socialise. I became so obsessed about all the negatives of this situation that I lost sight of the big picture.

It was this event that made me start to realise and identify how, throughout my life and in many business situations, I had allowed obsession to get the better of me. I began to reassess all the times when dragging my gaze away from the bright, shiny thing (in this case the sun ... never a good idea to look at that for too long) and seeing the bigger picture would have saved or improved situations both in work and in life.

I have learned that obsessions do not have to be a long-term or life-consuming thing either; like my mini, pop-up obsession about the CBD event, they can come fleetingly. They can take over your life or can take over a moment. It can be a situation that we struggle with, a specific outcome that we want to control, a person that we have a love/hate relationship with, a celebrity that we are intrigued by but also resent at the same time, a one-sided love interest, plastic surgery, video games or even social media.

Obsession can be a momentary thing, a mindset we cannot let go or a kind of addiction that controls our mind and soul … although I will say, real addiction is something else entirely and too big an issue to deal with here, and if you think you have an addiction please don't wait, get help now.

Whether it's big or small, an obsession is a fantasy castle we build for ourselves. We look at it through rose-tinted glasses, not seeing that it leaves everything else in our lives in shadow. The reality is never what we think. But believe me, I get it, as you have seen. In the thrall of obsessions, we shut out the full spectrum of experiences, choices and opportunities, and our obsession becomes a solitary spotlight focused on an ideal. We take a simple experience in life and amplify it into an object of disproportionate importance. We lose ourselves and who we are in a futile attempt to save ourselves from reality.

When I was in my early twenties I had an obsession with having a Louis Vuitton weekend bag. At that time, I was on a tight student budget and I couldn't afford it. Working for a magazine at the time opened my eyes to the luxury of designer pieces and, naturally, I mooned over the ads in that magazine and others, admiring those iconic Louis

Vuitton campaigns. The fact that they featured powerful and strong women carrying that bag was catnip to me. I created a fantasy in my mind that once I was able to afford that bag, my life would be perfect, because I too would be a powerful and strong woman with a Louis Vuitton bag. All I cared about was working hard and earning enough to buy that bag. It became my totem of success.

Spin on a few years and I am 25. Each month I paid my rent and my bills and put a little aside and, now, trembling at the handbag counter as the till rang out and the card machine beeped its approval, I had finally bought the bag of my dreams. I was exhilarated, I worked hard and it felt good! I was now a member of that club of strong, powerful and successful women who are able to carry a Louis Vuitton weekend bag and jet off on a luxury weekend to St-Tropez, Ibiza or the Hamptons. I was powerful, I was strong, I had made it ... hear me roar!

Well, that feeling lasted for a couple of weeks. Then I realised I was basically the exact same person, but now I was a person with a bag that was making my shoes look bad. The bag was just a bag. There was no secret Louis Vuitton owners' power club. I hadn't been given a corner office, and I had the sneaking feeling that if I had not scrimped so much and instead had spent the money on going out after work, enjoying myself, getting my personality out there and buying the boss a round of drinks, I might have got noticed and promoted faster. It was a hollow victory that in the end, gave me nothing ... except a bag.

We all have obsessions, good and bad. Having the clarity and presence of mind to identify the bad ones is the key. And it's not always about wishing for success or some other life-improving goal. You may be super-successful already and have achieved everything that you wanted in your life, but there is still one small thing that you are obsessed about. The obsession may equate to 5 per cent of what is going on in your life but in your mind you give it an importance of 95 per cent. The balance is out of whack and all of a sudden everything begins to topple.

I have given you two examples of when an obsession skewed my happiness ... and believe me, there have been many others. To go through all of them would be tedious for you and sobering for me, but I hope the above has given you an idea of what I mean when I talk about obsession. Enough about me ... what about you? Do you have an obsession that is getting in the way of your best life? How do you even identify that you have an obsession? Well, the first thing to do is admit you have one! As I have described, it's perfectly fine to determinedly go after a goal or to be a super-fan of something or somebody, but is there something currently in your life that even you have thought, 'Hmm, I'm thinking/talking/tweeting about this a bit toooo much!'? Well, if there is, then try my super-duper 'Am I Obsessed?' test.

Write down the thing that you are constantly thinking about, and this should be the one thing you feel is key to attaining happiness, or is coming between you and your happiness. Write down every detail you can about it and be honest about how it makes you feel in all phases of engagement, that is, before, during and after whatever it is. I can only generalise here ... some will be physical, some mental. The important thing to do is acknowledge all the ways it makes you feel. Usually a negative obsession will drain us of our power, making us feel weak, depleted and very much unhappy, but there may be flashes of joy, like when I got my bag, but they are outweighed by the negative.

Once you have identified the obsession and admitted how it makes you feel, write down a moment in your life before that obsession started and you felt you were aligned with your highest power, a time when you felt on top of the world and were happy. Feel that feeling. Is this obsession of yours coming between you and your highest self? Is it stopping you from having that feeling again? Write down the feelings you get from that moment of your highest self and compare them with the feelings you get from chasing that obsession. Is this obsession making your life better or worse?

Are you seeing this obsession through rose-tinted glasses? Once you have everything down on paper, weigh up the pros and cons and you may just see that you do indeed have an obsession. One that is preventing you from being happy.

When we have an obsession, we hand over our power to it. When you hand over your power, you hand over control of your own happiness. You are no longer able to be happy when left to your own devices because you put all your hopes on being happy into that obsession. In order for you to get back to your state of being in control, and aligned with who you are, you need to get rid of that obsession. Or at least develop a healthier relationship with it.

So how do you overcome an obsession? Letting go is a process, so don't beat yourself up. It takes time and it will not happen overnight. Here are some steps to get you started.

How to Live Your Best Life Secret #6

10 steps for letting go of an obsession

Whether it's a person, a celebrity, plastic surgery or a video game, obsessions can take over our lives. Getting over an obsession is not an easy task, it takes time and a lot of back and forth until you are truly over it. Don't beat yourself up if you can't get rid of it immediately. Take baby steps and you will get there. These are ten steps to help you work on getting over an obsession:

1. Distance yourself from the object of your obsession. Obsession with a person is a sign of an unhealthy relationship. Physical distance creates mental distance. If you impose distance the obsession will start to weaken. If it's an obsession over a pastime or a video game, disconnect the console, sell your kit, give it away to a friend, or at the very least put it into storage where you can't easily get it. If it's social media-related, delete the app(s) from your phone and disconnect from it for a while.

2. Stop feeding it. Feeding an obsession will give you an instant hit of dopamine and it's hard to break the habit. You have to starve it. If, for instance, it's an obsession with a celebrity, stop looking at their social media and thinking that you are living their life or are befriending them. The more mental

space you give this obsession, the more control it will have over you.

3. Find a distraction. Distracting yourself from obsessive thoughts is easier said than done. It's hard to stop thinking about your obsession as it feels so good to think and talk about it. But remember why you want to get rid of this obsession in the first place: it is so you can enjoy all the other things in life. When you are overtaken by obsessive thoughts, find some easy ways to distract yourself such as working out, reading, talking to a friend (about anything other than your obsession) or focusing on your work. NB: Don't just replace one obsession with another!

4. Be in the moment. If you are always daydreaming about your obsession, your mind is never where your body is. You may be living another life in your mind and missing important moments with your family, friends or work. Find ways to be in the moment. Meditation, yoga or connecting with nature all help. Engage in conversations: when people talk to you listen carefully to what they are saying rather than daydreaming or trying to shoehorn in a chat about your obsession. Try to focus. Or find a mantra that keeps you in the moment: 'I am here, I am present.'

5. Form new habits. If you are obsessed over one person, try to meet new people and form new relationships. Becoming closer to others makes you realise how much more the world has to offer compared to that one obsession. Even if the

obsession is not a person, meeting new people will introduce you to new ideas and perspectives.

6. Learn a new skill or take up a new hobby. It's easier said than done, again, but you will be making new connections and memories, and finding excitement outside the object of your obsession.

7. Change your daily habits. At times we can't distance ourselves from our obsession as we have incorporated it into our daily routines. Ask yourself which routines can be shaken up if they are keeping you attached to your obsession. You probably know the answer right away. Try to change your routines and your obsessive thoughts will weaken before too long. Routine changes can be as simple as not checking social media first thing when you wake up, taking on a meditation practice instead or taking a long break during the day. You could try taking a different route to work and going to different hangout spots to avoid seeing someone you are obsessed with.

8. Refresh your life. Take back control by making some personal changes. Identify the things that remind you of your obsession and do something else to renew and refresh your life.

9. Talk to a therapist. Sometimes an obsession runs so deep that it's impossible to get rid of it by yourself. Speaking to a therapist will get it out of your mind and help you ground it. A therapist should give you the tools to regain control of your thoughts and take charge of your life again.

10. Don't let the obsession take over. It's up to you to know if your obsession is manageable. If it brings you joy and you can still enjoy the rest of your life, then it's not the sort of thing I am talking about here. If that's the case you can keep it up until it runs its course, but if it's fully taking over, then it's up to you to make a decision to cut it off and take control of your life again. It's going to be baby steps perhaps, but know that all obsessions ultimately fade out and so will yours; it's just a matter of time. However, by being proactive you can beat it and live your best life now!

7

Don't
Compare
and
Despair

In the rarefied world of beauty-brand founders, I am a bit of an outsider. Most founders of recent, successful beauty brands are makeup artists or facialists or plastic surgeons. They already have a history, experience and a reputation in the beauty industry, so their path to launching a product seems to be a natural progression. I am very different, from the point of view that my only connection with beauty was having spent a couple of years as a beauty writer for a teen magazine while I was at uni. Not exactly the credentials that would naturally lead me to launch a legitimate beauty brand ... at least not on paper, but as any decent guide to entrepreneurs will tell you, I did have one or two essential ingredients. I had passion and I had a vision. I knew exactly how my brand would be different to everyone else out there and I doggedly pursued that dream until I made it come true. I won't go into that saga here, other than to say if you really want to know the gripping story, you should buy my first two books ... available online and at all good bookstores! Ah, the entrepreneurial spirit never leaves you! But no amount of passion or belief could hide the fact that I didn't really have a background in beauty, and I always had a bit of an issue with that. I felt like I was a lightweight and, when compared to all the other founders of beauty brands, founders with the 'right' background and the right credentials, I would be found wanting.

When I first launched Rodial, I hired one of the most reputable agencies in London to execute the PR launch. They knew their stuff and got me and my new brand into places and in front of people I would have had no chance of reaching otherwise. One of those meetings was with the beauty director of *Harper's Bazaar* magazine in London. She had been in the industry all her life and was very well respected, so yes, it was a little daunting, but I had got my pitch down, we had a great product and I was full of energy and enthusiasm.

My PR and I were invited to her office (for what is known as a 'deskside meeting') to present my new range. We said hello, and I went into my tried and trusted opening bit about my journey, why I started the brand and how it was different to everything else on the market. It's a good story and I had told it many times – we were getting smiles and nods. All good. On to part two of the presentation. This is the bit where we would start opening jars and do all the touchy-freely stuff, sampling the gorgeous textures, smelling the product and admiring the packaging – this was always a winner. In every presentation so far, this is where the 'oohs' and 'ahs' would happen, this was where we won the sale, and it worked pretty much every time. Pretty much. This was not to be one of those times.

As I reached for a sample I was stopped in my tracks by a challenging series of very detailed, intricate, technical questions about the product, the technology used, the chemical ratios and a host of other things. My mouth fell open, I stuttered, I blustered and the smiles from the other side of the desk were now noticeably lacking. As I said, she had been in the beauty industry for years, so she knew her retinols from her copper peptides and I was floundering … badly. I mean, I had personally come up with these ideas, and had developed all the products working with an amazing lab. I knew the basics, but I was no chemist. They could tell you every percentage of every ingredient, but I hadn't thought I needed to know all those answers myself. How very wrong I was. The meeting ended there, and with hot, prickly embarrassment we packed up and headed out. I felt dazed and deflated. I will never, ever forget that meeting. My PR tried to make me feel better, but I felt horrible and was ready to give it all up there and then. What was I doing setting myself up as a beauty brand? I knew nothing!

Looking back now, I realise that I was having a flash of 'imposter syndrome'. It can strike anyone at any time, but it's particularly common in high achievers. It's that feeling that you really aren't up to this, and you are going to be found out. You start to believe you only got this far not because of your skills or talents, but through dumb luck, or because you were in the right place at the right time, or because other people liked you. You tell yourself that you don't really deserve this, you don't belong here ... you are an imposter.

The syndrome was identified in the late seventies and was initially only thought to affect women, but research has proven that men can suffer from it too, although women do tend to be more susceptible. In addition, as Clare Josa states in her book *Ditching Imposter Syndrome*, men tend to suffer less as they harness their confidence-boosting testosterone reserves and power through the self-doubt, whereas women tend to give in to it. And to cap it all, what group is most likely to suffer from imposter syndrome? Female entrepreneurs. Obvs.

Imposter syndrome can be a real block to success, whether you are trying to make it on your own or fit in with a company. It holds you back from speaking up at the meeting, it stops you from making that call, it means you don't push for a pay rise. In the long run, it's not only bad for the individual, it's bad for the economy ... all those potentially brilliant business ideas and female CEOs are being stifled by this lack of confidence and fear, but even if you do make it to the top of the tree, it can still affect you. I know several high-flyers who, instead of seeing themselves as others see them, still put their success down to luck, and feel they have somehow cheated their way to the top.

After that meeting I was overcome by negative thoughts: 'You don't know what you are doing', 'What made you think you'd be any good at this', 'You are a failure and a fraud.' It was tough and I really didn't know how to get out of it. Gradually, by focusing on all the things I knew I was good at, the things I knew only I could do, I was able to build myself back up and shake off those feelings.

So, it will come as no shock to learn that I didn't give up that day, but I did learn every detail about every one of my products from then on. I learned what was in the tube, what the tube was made of, where the cardboard for the box was sourced, what the delivery-truck driver's kid was called and what football team he supported. I knew it all. I realised I did belong here: I had a great brand and knew how to market it and no one else had done what I was doing.

Years later, that very first fear came back to haunt me. In the intervening years we had launched Rodial makeup to sit alongside the skincare and beauty lines and it was becoming a big part of the brand. Also in that time, a little social media thing called Instagram had started up ... you may have heard of it. Recently, there has been a big trend on Instagram for makeup beauty-brand founders to record mini video tutorials on how they apply makeup. What better way to sell a product than to see the creator actually using the product on themselves, giving insider tips and showing the transformation. They always looked perfect and, as I watched one after the other, the same rising irrationalities came back to haunt me. Not only was I being dragged down by imposter syndrome, but watching these Insta makeover videos was starting to become an obsession too. Double whammy!

I was starting to feel like I didn't belong in the industry any more. I mean, this is obviously the new way of doing things, the videos are getting millions of likes, so it's obviously what the people want ... but what can I do? My makeup skills were pretty basic, to be honest, and so I would look like an absolute idiot if I tried to do my makeup on camera. On top of that, it wasn't even my vibe: I spend about five minutes in the morning doing my makeup as I prioritise other things, like meditation, family, working out, researching and, well, when else do you think I have the time to write three books? It appeared that some of these makeup artists spend about an hour making themselves up, and on top of that many of the videos seemed to have pro-lighting, graphics and all manner of slick things that frankly I didn't have the time or the interest to replicate. But my obsession and feelings of inadequacy would not let it go: the more I obsessively watched the videos, the more I worried that this was now the industry norm and if I wasn't doing a makeup video we'd be left behind. But if I did do one then everyone would be able to tell I was out of my depth ... I'd be found out. Uh-oh! That sounds familiar.

I could see where this was heading and recalled how I came back from that *Harper's Bazaar* car crash. So, I decided to unfollow every single beauty-brand account there and then (apart from my own!). No time limits, no gradual detox, just quick, decisive action. I had come to realise that by following these accounts, I was just compounding my feelings of inadequacy by comparing myself to them. Obsessively watching what they were doing just made me focus on the fact that I wasn't doing the same and made me feel bad. By looking at those accounts, I fixed the idea in my mind that there was only one path to success, i.e. the path that all these other brands were following and, as I wasn't keeping up, I wasn't enough. Not healthy.

So, when I stopped following them, I achieved two things. First of all, I cleared my head from all this clutter. It was like emerging from darkness in to light ... I could suddenly see everything clearly. Have you ever had one of those days when you accidently leave your phone at home? You know it's safe, so you don't have the panic that comes from losing it, and after the initial feeling of being cast adrift, it starts to feel quite freeing. Well, it was like that, only more so. And once I was free, that led to the second thing: I was able to focus on the ways I was different to everyone else. In this instance, I was different because I was connecting with my followers in a different way, a way that said exactly what I needed to say about my brand and myself. I shared all the stuff you'd expect about new launches and what stuff is going on behind the scenes at work, but I also loved sharing motivational quotes and lessons learned from challenges in business, so instead of trying to mimic what others were doing, I just did more of what I was doing. And you know what, it worked. I got a lot of new followers, my existing followers responded even more, and we built a wonderful community. I was thrilled to discover that by putting it out there that, even though I run a beauty and makeup brand, I don't care about taking an hour every morning to apply my face, there is a big community of like-minded people, people who still use beauty and makeup products but don't obsess about the perfect smoky eye. This is my community, this is my niche and this is the audience I speak to ... and I love them.

During lockdown and as part of getting out of my comfort zone, I had to find a way to 'speak to our audience'. I wasn't doing speeches and personal appearances any more, so social media was all I had. Ironically, I started posting a few Instagram stories every day on my @mrsrodial account with my skincare tips and (basic) makeup tutorials. I said to myself, 'These only last for 24 hours and if they are terrible, they will be deleted for ever.' I thought they would completely flop but I was surprised to find a lot of regular people (i.e. not professional makeup artists or beauty industry insiders) related to my style and gave me great feedback. That gave me confidence to continue do more of what I had been dreading for years. I got used to seeing myself on camera and the sound of my own voice (no one likes the sound of their voice, I hear). You still won't see me delivering a 'Perfect 30-minute Smoky Eye Tutorial' but, instead, as I always do, I present the real me and share all my everyday skin and makeup tips in my own style. I am putting myself out there my way, and it seems to work after all!

So, to get back to our main topic, it doesn't have to be a full-blown imposter syndrome that holds you back. As the title of this chapter suggests, something as simple as comparing yourself to your peers can make you unhappy (unless when you compare yourself you think you are actually superior to everybody else; that's another syndrome entirely!). It's the times that you start to compare yourself with friends or colleagues at work, for instance, that lead to unhappiness. You can be sure that whatever worries you have about your perceived imperfections will grow quickly, not least because you are seeing these people all the time, and that goes double if you are also constantly checking them out on social media. You come back from work, feeling a bit down on yourself, you feel you are lacking inspiration and this is what you are seeing: one of your workmates is about to go on an exotic holiday when you only managed a wet weekend in Morecambe; the other just had an expensive face and body makeover and is looking amazing, and you look, well ... not amazing. Someone else is having a luxurious meal, you are opening a second bag of crisps for dinner, and so it goes on, an endless bombardment of perfect holidays, perfect relationships, perfect faces, perfect bodies. And beyond the people you actually know are those you follow who seem to be endlessly on free press trips or unboxing free clothes and gifts. How does all this make you feel? Worthless? Questioning why and how these people are getting all the perks and you get nothing, even though you work as hard as they do, maybe even harder? You question your self-worth. You may feel that you don't have anyone to support you. You can't help but compare yourself and wonder. This makes you unhappy.

You look at those amazing bodies they have. You say to yourself, I will only be happy if I have that body, and to have that body I need to go to that expensive gym and book that personal trainer. I don't have the budget for that therefore I can't have a great body, and if I haven't got a great body then I can't wear designer outfits, and without designer outfits I won't get the likes on social media, and without the followers on social media no one will pay attention to me and I'll never get any celeb friends, and without any celeb friends I'll never live the successful life I want to be living ... if only I could afford that gym. You convince yourself that your lack of resources is at the root of all your problems. That's just one example. There are, of course, a host of comparison scenarios and blame-game spirals I could have chosen.

Comparison is a common human dynamic, so I'm not saying you shouldn't ever allow yourself to do it. That would be crazy and probably impossible, unless you have somehow achieved some kind of seventh-level, Zen Buddhist enlightenment and are at one with the universe. We are always going to compare ourselves to others in all areas of our lives. Consciously and unconsciously we are constantly sizing up the competition: who's got the better job, more money, higher social status, better-looking boyfriend/girlfriend; who's got the picture-perfect life. This is a natural human behaviour and it helps us get inspired, learn, define and improve ourselves. It gives us a compass bearing on our life's journey and to gauge how we are doing and sometimes even feel better about ourselves if we see we are doing better than others ... school reunions can be useful in this regard. But as I want to highlight here, and I am sure we all have felt from time to time, it can also be pretty stressful and make us more competitive than we need to be.

So, this natural human inclination has been going on forever: your cave is better than my cave, how come they get invited to Caesar's orgy and I don't, why did Leonardo paint that misery guts Mona Lisa and not me? I mean, I've got a proper smile with teeth and everything. And so on down the ages of mankind. But recently our deep-seated comparative instincts have been super-charged to a whole new level by the introduction of ... yep, you guessed it ... social media.

We compare our everyday lives with other people's, but instead of seeing a real person we are seeing a curated feed and we never quite know if they are actually spontaneous moments and these people really are super-cool and effortlessly stylish, or if we are being fed a rigorously edited narrative designed to portray a picture-perfect life to the outside world. Was that perfect image you just liked really a beautifully spontaneous snatched moment on the beach that they just had to share? Or was it staged as part of an all-day shoot with a crew of 30 production staff and happened to be the image that, out of the 800 shots taken that day, best represented the brand ideals of the yoga pants the person you are following 'just happened' to be wearing?

And it's not just experiences and material goods that we covet and compare. It can also hurt our relationships when we compare ourselves to the ideal ones we see online. We all know *that* couple, right? They bombard us with posts that are #loved-up, #blessed and #couplegoals personified, and if it isn't posts gushing about loving relationships that would put Romeo and Juliet in the shade, then it's posts about family ... super-talented kids and cherubic, non-puking, soundly sleeping babies. (Mumsnet regularly goes to town on this and it is not pretty!)

So, we scroll and scroll, and even the most enlightened of us can become affected by what the feed reveals. We see who is doing what and we note that we're not doing any of this stuff, our husband hasn't said anything vaguely romantic in weeks, never mind given you anything to attach a hashtag to, and the kids are seemingly some feral sub-breed of human. It's no wonder we get stressed out wondering if we are doing enough, earning enough or enjoying life enough.

This is causing a lot of people anxiety and makes us question the quality of our own relationships. I had a serious Harry and Meghan phase for a while. I mean, beautiful actress meets dashing, action-man prince and he gives up the royal palaces and titles to protect their love ... Come on! How can we measure up to that? We are all susceptible: we are looking at the online, curated feed of a couple or family that is presented as the shining ideal, then we look at our own and there is no way ours can measure up.

Research has shown that our online posting habits are directly related to our need for 'relationship visibility' – the extent to which we make our relationships part of our public personas. A very high relationship visibility and over-posting about a partner can often indicate a masking of relationship insecurity. Simply put, people who need more reassurance about their relationship will post more about it. For example, they feel they are not getting reassurance from their partner, so they take a relationship picture and post it on Instagram for likes. They are looking for positive attention when they are not getting what they want from the relationship. There are instances where the posts may just be for show, it's all about looking picture-perfect, setting the right image and getting the approval of their peers, but it's not really a meaningful relationship. Others may feel they have something to prove or want to take the focus off other areas in their lives they feel insecure about. It's important to know that all relationships have their ups and downs and no one is going to post a picture of a fight or disagreement with their partner, or comment about taking out the recycling, or when the stairs need hoovering or when things are just a bit dull. No relationship is as perfect as it looks on Instagram so always remember to take it with a pinch of salt.

Actually, the curated lifestyle phenomenon isn't entirely new. Before Instagram we would compare our lives and our scatter cushions to the ones we saw in *Hello!* magazine. The gossip mags of the 1920 and 1930s movie scene were full of similar 'ideal couples' and glamourous lifestyles. The studios would set up staged 'at home' shoots to promote a star, or fix up couples they thought would work well together for the movie-going public. Quite often the paired-up stars detested each other, were really seeing other people or the 'relationship' was set up to put people off the scent if a movie star was gay. They would be 'surprised' at an intimate dinner or out on the town by Hollywood snappers (what we would now call the paparazzi) and the story would run in the various glossy mags. The public would lap up the story of romance and lavish lifestyles, and the image would be complete. It was a set-up then, and it's a set-up now. For a brilliant and highly entertaining reference to all this, see *Singin' in the Rain* with Gene Kelly and Debbie Reynolds or the Coen brothers' *Hail Caesar!*

OK, back to today. I've spoken about how comparing ourselves to others can hurt us generally, and how this is not a new thing, but I believe it is the social media aspect of this that has led to a ramping up of the problem.

By comparing yourself to others online, you are distracting yourself from your best moments in life: the average person spends two hours a day on social media, resulting in fewer real accomplishments, reduced interpersonal interaction and a constant sense that we don't have enough time. We start saying no to things that can positively affect our mental health like fitness, socialising and education, convincing ourselves that these are not a priority. Too much social media can also mean we are:

Absorbing negativity: social media is a platform for arguments, fake news, negativity and bullying that can make us angry and upset on a daily basis. Repeated exposure to this negativity can make it feel like we are living in a world full of hatred, chaos and rage, which can lead to depression over time.

Receiving unwanted attention: sharing too much of our lives can invite unwelcome attention. We lower our boundaries; other people think they know us and have opinions or expectations of us that are unrealistic or hurtful.

Isolating ourselves without even realising it: living our life on social media, we far too often step away from those who are right in front of us in order to attend to those who are not present. I've been to many a party where I've watched guests spend most of the time posting about it on Instagram rather than actually being in the moment and enjoying it. Not for them the joy of a hug and a good conversation. Nope. It's all about finding the right backdrop and hogging the full-length mirror, then they sit hunched on a kitchen stool editing and adding filters for an hour before doing it all again. People are props, fun is marketable, life is meaningless.

Getting addicted: we may all get caught up in the need to 'perform' on social media. The need to create and maintain an online persona that takes too much of our time in real life – 'If I don't post every day I'll lose followers, etc., etc.' It can become a bit of an obsession. The constant need to create content is a real pressure, you feel you need to keep upping the ante. Reality shows are always creating dramas out of nothing for exactly the same reason ... but getting addicted to performing on social media will drag you down in the end.

As I said, it is natural to make some comparisons, but when the images we see of seemingly perfect lives are everywhere, it can be a real battle. Living this way can affect your peace and happiness. Often, beneath the need to compare, is a deep-rooted sense that we are not enough. We feel that we lack something, and we project that on to others so we don't feel bad about ourselves.

How to Live Your Best Life Secret #7

10 ways to stop the comparison game

If you find yourself feeling constantly unsettled by comparing yourself to your peers, especially when you follow them on social media, it is important that you get yourself out of that state of mind. Here are some ways to train your brain and to help you care less about other people's lives on social media:

1. Remove yourself. While you may not be able to remove yourself entirely from social media, you can mute any accounts that are causing you the most distress. Remember, you don't need to be on social media every day to know what's going on with your friends. It's OK to check social media every couple of days, once a week or once in a while – whatever feels good for you. Distance yourself from accounts that make you feel inferior or that make you want things that you can't have.

2. Create an intention or purpose. Your intention could be connecting with friends, doing research or getting inspiration. Creating an intention keeps you focused on your purpose for the account and could prevent the idle social media comparisons that happen when you start to mindlessly wander. You would also be less vulnerable to triggers that make you feel bad about yourself and your life.

3. Change your perspective. There are two ways to look at social media feeds: we can choose to see the negative and damaging or the positive and non-threatening. When you see a friend and a new project they've completed, you can choose to be jealous or you can choose to be happy and inspired by their success. Choose the positive perspective and be happy for them. Viewing things from a positive perspective creates a positive mindset. This way you are more likely to find joy, inspiration and light when you go on social media.

4. Assess your attitude. In a world of selfies and narcissism, it's easy to think you deserve attention and praise. We have all seen very average, unremarkable pictures that somehow have a million likes, while your superb post is only getting three, and of those one is from your mum and one is from her dog. Someone's filtered picture with its smart caption and a few hashtags thrown in there getting all the love can make your head boil with envy. The truth is that you don't deserve attention just because you want it. Check your ego and don't let it take over. Other people's success isn't your failure. Be happy for that person and move on.

5. Define happiness on social media. Getting a bunch of likes on Instagram doesn't make you happy. You'll get an instant dopamine boost, but then you'll crave more attention and likes once this has worn off. The cycle never ends. Focus on being successful

in your own way, offline and outside social media, and know that for every perfect picture post there are probably a lot of darker things happening in the background.

6. Replace social media. Find other things to fill your time instead of constantly focusing on social media. Read a book, go online for research on topics that are of interest to you, listen to a podcast, watch a TED Talk. There are lots of entertaining things that you can do instead of scrolling down social media for hours.

7. Find role models. Choose who you follow on social media and follow role models and people who inspire you: people you can genuinely learn from and benefit from their success without adding an element of competitiveness. It's easier to learn from a role model like Oprah Winfrey or Bill Gates rather than a friend from real life. You don't personally know them and likely never will, and they are so distant from you that it's impossible to compare. You will never worry about them judging your outfit when you bump into each other on the school run.

8. Create a support network. Create a supportive circle of friends outside social media who you genuinely care for and who support each other. The type of people who don't brag about their lives on social media. Establish a true offline connection with them.

9. Practise gratitude. When you find yourself comparing your life to others or feeling resentful of someone

else's success, think of three things that you are proud of. Re-create the feeling that you felt when you achieved them and feel good about them. Stay in that frame of mind, celebrating and appreciating what you have rather than focusing on what you're missing.

10. Remember that *you* are in charge. In the end, you are responsible for your emotions. Not Facebook, not Instagram, not Twitter, not TikTok or any other form of social media that has been invented between me writing this and you reading it: it's you. You can help manage your emotions by staying in control, regardless of any negative influences. You can control who sees your posts, who can and cannot comment, you can remove something or someone if you don't like what you see, you can block or mute someone and you can accept or reject a connection request. Follow your own path and remember where you started. Instead of comparing yourself to others, simply compare yourself to you two years ago and just see how far you've come!

8

Own Your
Energy

You are happy when you control the energy of a situation in a positive way. There are a lot of times that we know we are right and we know that the other side is not, and our ego wants to win. I like to win. I mean, no one wants to lose, do they? Especially when you know deep down that you are right. Pierre de Coubertin, the father of the modern Olympic games may have said, 'The important thing in life is not to triumph, but to compete', but he also instigated giving a gold medal to the winner … so, yeah, winning is best. However, I believe that quote, as well as being a great motto for motivation and self-belief, also guides us towards the concept of winning, and losing, with grace. In sport we celebrate not only the winners, but the plucky underdog, the triers, the good sports, and tend to reject a gloating, ungracious champion. Winning is great, but I believe how you win is more important. So it is in life and in business, where for me the arena is more often a meeting room or PR phone call. You will raise your points, put up an argument, play your best game and the other side will do that too, but, in life, it's worth questioning what is more important: winning or keeping the relationship?

December 2015. This is a big deal. We are working with Kylie Jenner in LA and, like the CBD event, I spend a lot of time trying to block out the constant 'tick, tick, tick' of the expenses meter running in my head. We had previously worked with Kylie in London (the full story on working with Kylie Jenner is in my book *How to Be an Overnight Success*), and that took a lot, but this was a much bigger expense as we had to fly the whole team over … all our talent and resources, lock, stock and barrel, all on the clock. As my accountants often point out in meetings, 'We are not L'Oréal, we are a small private company, with limited budget!' This *has* to be money well spent and, to be honest, I am confident it will be. The London event with Kylie did wonders for the brand and we got great coverage, so I am sure this will do the same. Nevertheless, it is quite stressful. I am mentally calculating the cost of every bottle of water and every resulting loo break.

Of course, as this is a high-profile, celeb-centric, beauty PR event, curveballs are flying in thick and fast, including a two-hour delay while we scoured California and a significant part of Arizona to source extra 'special' hair extensions when the stylist suddenly announced she needed more to achieve the look she wanted. Now, this wasn't my first rodeo, and one should always expect this sort of delay to happen on a shoot, so I had built time into the schedule to allow for this sort of thing. I had built precisely two hours into the schedule, in fact ... so now we are up against it. Everything else has to go like clockwork for us to hit our deadline. We have interviews and calls lined up with journalists and beauty reviewers from all over the world, all dialling in from different time zones. We can't miss a single one. Then, assuming that all goes well, the whole travelling circus moves to a different location (the W Hollywood hotel) for the press photo call.

Tensions are running high, but we have done it. The shoot at Studio City could not have gone better, the calls have all happened, and we are on schedule for the move to the W Hollywood.

Before we head out, Kylie has an outfit change for the shoot. She will be wearing a beautiful black and white David Koma dress. Now, the way this works is that stylists call up the designer's PR agent and say, 'Oh, I am the stylist for this person and they are up for an Oscar/appearing as a judge on TV/doing a PR shoot for a cool product, and can we borrow a dress?' Depending on the brand and the celeb involved, this is great for the designer as they get free publicity and it's great for us as we get the loan of a spectacular dress. After the shoot, the stylist returns the dress to the PR agency and it is ready for its next close-up. Some dresses have a more packed and glamourous schedule than the celebs whose shoulders they are draped over: *Vogue* cover shoot one day, then on to a red-carpet event the next! They hang out with, or rather on, supermodels and movie stars at exclusive parties, awards ceremonies, movie premieres and fashion weeks … Actually, is it possible to be reincarnated as a dress?

So, back to the plot. Kylie is now dressed and on her way to the W when one of my team comes and tells me that Kylie would like to wear the dress that evening on a date with Tyga. We have arranged for it to be worn for the shoot then carefully packed and sent back to David Koma, but Kylie loves it so much she wants to wear it to go out to Nobu after the shoot. Basically, for this to happen, the rules say we have to buy the dress. Everyone looks at me … my company, my decision. That ticking money meter in my head is now spinning wildly out of control. This is a dress costing several thousand dollars. What are the options here? How do I win?

What happens if we say no? I save myself several thousand dollars, but that might create a bad energy and mood on the shoot, when I need everyone to be working as a team. If I say yes I am blowing money that could pay someone's salary for a few months. It's money that I could have used for marketing, to design packaging for a new product or to update our flagship counter. I'd rather do any of those things rather than throw the money away on a few pieces of fabric (admittedly a very beautiful and expertly crafted few pieces of fabric) that will not help the business or add to the campaign in any way.

We talk. Kylie just wants to wear it to Nobu, that's it – we'll still have to buy the dress for that to happen, but after she has worn it out on the town she won't wear it again, so she will hand it back to us. We have found a middle ground we can agree on. Making sacrifices is important to keep certain relationships, but finding a middle ground is the best way forward. Kylie goes away happy, she looks fabulous at Nobu that night, and I get to keep something as a memento of the campaign and the time we worked with Kylie. Who knows what that could mean in the future? As I write, the $6 plastic crown that Biggie Smalls wore for a magazine shoot just went for over half a million dollars at a Sotheby's auction.

From my perspective, the cost of that dress on top of what we had already spent on that campaign and bringing everyone over nearly drove me crazy. It was right on the edge of being another CBD party episode, but I looked at the pros and cons coolly and calmly. It was a wedge of money, but it wasn't going to take us out of business. I reasoned that from their perspective, asking a brand if you can keep the dress after a shoot probably isn't a big issue. The model may do it quite often, and if they are dealing with big brands then they are probably used to getting an instant 'Yes, no problem.' If I had said an outright 'No' it would have risked making them feel uncomfortable, creating negative energy, and, as I looked at things from their angle, it would have made us look small-time. My version of a win was to keep all parties happy and keep the energy positive.

Seeing the other side's point of view and trying to find a solution that wasn't 100 per cent what we wanted but kept everything positive, not only helped to save the day and keep us all happy, but when we wanted to work with Kylie and her sisters again, the relationship was still friendly and we were able to do more great things together. If we had put up a huge fight about that dress, we could have created bad energy. Saying yes was an investment in a future relationship ... one that benefits both parties. Burning bridges is never a good idea.

This was what I call the 'Solution of the Highest Good', even though it may not be the solution that we are aligned with at the time. There always is a 'Highest Good' if you look for it. This is easier to accept when things are going your way but when there is a challenge, the ego wants to take over and we look for other people and things to blame. A Solution of the Highest Good keeps the energy positive ... it keeps it flowing and maintains the positive relationship between the different parties.

I recently faced a personal challenge to this philosophy when I decided to go house-hunting. We'd been in our old place for quite a while and, although moving house is apparently one of the top three 'most traumatic life events', I took a deep breath and dived headlong into the cut and thrust of the London property market. Now, I don't know if I struck lucky or the tales of woe and gnashing of teeth I had heard from friends and colleagues who had recently moved were exaggerated, but within a very short time I found what I thought was the ideal house. Style, tick, location, tick, price, tick. So, I quickly made an appointment to view it. My husband was busy, so I went to see it on my own as we couldn't afford to hang about, and I'd report back to him if there were any issues. Basically, if it was as good in the flesh as it looked on paper. We were pretty much agreed that this was the one we wanted. I paused at the gate ... if anything, it looked better than the pictures. I was very excited and internally chanting a mantra of 'please don't be sold, please don't be sold' as I walked up to the front door.

I knocked, the door opened, and I was caught completely off guard, not by the house, but by the owner. It was someone I knew! She wasn't a close friend (I'm pretty sure I know where my best friends actually live) but someone I had met a few times and was in the same circle of friends as me and my other half. After we got over the initial bafflement and nervous laughter, she showed me around and the house was all I hoped ... I loved it. I knew I definitely wanted this house, so as soon as I was out of the door I put in an offer. And, as I didn't want any messing about, I put in the offer at the asking price. I felt sure that this, combined with the fact that we knew each other, would mean I'd be moving in next week. I began planning paint colours in my mind.

The next morning the estate agent rang as expected. I opened my diary in anticipation of a moving date, but that is not what the call was about. 'Erm ... I'm afraid she doesn't want to sell the house to you.' I didn't quite know what to say to this. 'Do you mean they want more money? We did offer the asking price, you know.' There was a moment's silence on the other end of the line. 'No, it's not about the money, the problem is you ... she doesn't want to sell the house to you ... I'm really sorry.'

To say I was shocked would be putting it mildly. I wracked my brains: what had I done? I've only met this woman a few times and now she seems to hate me so much she can't bear for me to be in the same building as her ... even after she's left it. What the hell is happening?

Finding out didn't do much to ease my feelings of utter disbelief. It turned out that my husband had been at a dinner party and they'd had a disagreement, and that was that. Now she refused to sell the house to me. I couldn't believe I was in this crazy situation. My first instinct was to go and tell her what a complete idiot she was and to bloody well grow up, but I quickly realised that was just my ego and my frustration trying to take over. I was not in control of the energy in this situation at all ... and so I needed to look at a way of making this work.

So, I got in touch with her direct. I just wanted to connect, have a chat, find out what was happening. I got no reply. I sent flowers asking again to meet, still nothing, but I persevered and eventually she agreed to meet with me. I knew I had to turn this around. I mean, regardless of the house, I hate the idea of someone not liking me ... particularly when it's not even my fault. I went in with no ego. I listened to her, I let her air all her grievances, she told me what she thought, I did not push back and, as we talked, we connected. We could get over this. By the time I left, we had found a middle ground and cleared the air. By going in with an open, ego-free attitude, rather than with both my hackles and my fists up, the tension was defused. She was able to tell me her side. I showed her I wasn't the person she thought and we both agreed that my husband could be a huge pain in the neck. Reader ... I got the house.

I found a solution by surrendering my ego and my agenda. In many situations, I have found that it's not about me winning the argument or reinforcing my point of view but that achieving a result that makes everyone happy is what really gives me the win. Let go of what you think you need, set a positive intention and let the universe guide you to the outcome of the highest good.

Just as we are affected by other people's energy, so our energy affects them. Our vibe contributes to the general energy of our surroundings. When you walk into a room and you are stressed out, you immediately bring down the energy; everyone around you can sense the tension and starts to feel uncomfortable. But when you enter a space with a peaceful and calm air, you project a grace and ambience that rubs off on everyone around you. I've seen this happen, I've felt this happen, and I am sure you will have too. Your energy is way more powerful than you think. You project your energy when you speak, when you smile, when you frown, in every aspect of your physical presence. I even feel the energy of emails from time to time ... lots of passive-aggressive stuff on there. I mean, everyone knows that 'Just checking in ...' really means, 'Hey, I already sent you one email about this and you didn't reply ...'; and 'I'll leave it with you ...' means. 'You're on your own with this cock-up' and so on. There is a lot of bad email energy around, so take care with your sign-offs! When you come from a fearful, low-energy state your thoughts and energy project that low energy around you, so conversely it makes sense that coming from a place of positive energy encourages everything around you to become more positive. If you want to raise the energy around you, take responsibility of your own energy first.

You get what you give. It's the law of attraction. Simply giving off certain energy will attract more of that energy back to you. If you feel abundant, you will attract more abundance. If you feel love, you will attract more love. So, if you're missing a certain energy from your life, ask yourself, 'Is there something I am not giving?'

How to Live Your Best Life Secret #8

10 ways to shift your energy to a positive state

1. Give up the attack thoughts. A common source of unhappiness is that we may be having a lot of 'attack thoughts', not just towards others but also turned in on ourselves. Even a small attack, such as a negative thought about the way we think we look or a nasty comment about another person, can all add up to a gradual pollution of our own energy.

2. Forgive. When you are unforgiving, you hold in anger, weakness, resentment. These create a low-level energy and block your ability to heal, grow and live your best life. Let go of pettiness, be the bigger person and don't forget to also forgive yourself.

3. Declutter your space, your home, your desk, your wardrobe. The feeling of cleanliness will also bring a fresh energy to your mind and your life.

4. Use compliments. It feels good to receive compliments but it's equally powerful to give them out. Giving out love and kindness can positively shift your energy and make you feel happier. When you give a genuine compliment, you can make someone's day and also reflect high vibes back on to yourself. Compliments have a ripple effect of positive energy … and that includes complimenting yourself!

5. Be the light, not the victim. When you are in a challenging situation, don't pity yourself; instead be

strong and behave towards the other party in the most positive way possible. Let go of your ego and be the light.

6. Send love. It's easy to send negative thoughts to people so you can protect yourself from being hurt. Judging others may give you temporary relief but it will be painful for you in the long run. Send mental love to everyone that you may have issues with: it could be a smile, a prayer, a positive thought. I often send loving thoughts to my office before I walk in.

7. Make time for what you love. Focus on what inspires you and find some time every week to do what you love. This will create positive energy . . . but don't allow it to become an obsession!

8. Welcome challenges as a way to learn. Also, seek out challenging people as your teachers. Ask yourself, 'What can I learn from this?' Your intuition will guide you to what you need to learn from every situation.

9. Don't add to the gossip. Cut off any negativity around you, don't add to the drama and gossip, and respond with silence and peace.

10. Write down what you like about yourself. At the beginning or the end of the day, write down three things you like about yourself. Do it every day and try to make them different. You will create a positive shift not only in how you feel but also in how you present yourself to the world, and as a bonus you will attract similar people and positive experiences into your life.

9

How to Live Your Best Life

Show up every day at 100 per cent your best. This is not a rehearsal, it is your life.

What if you woke up every day ready to live your best life? What if you were aligned with the woman (or man) you always wanted to be? What if you dressed like her, talked like her, attracted opportunities like her? What if you stepped into the power of the woman you are meant to be? What if you showed up feeling, looking and projecting your best? Nothing less.

How do you get there? You need to find the right shifts and steps in mindset to raise your vibration, build your confidence, elevate your thoughts, hone your vision and attract the best opportunities. Get fulfilled and excited about every single day. Go from feeling low-energy, overwhelmed and confused to aligned with your highest self and ready to take over the world. Be ready to level up every day.

How do we change our energy? Our energy is the vibe we are putting out to the world that shapes the quality of our experience. When we have high energy, we have positive thoughts, create a positive reality and we feel happy.

When I am stressed with work issues, I know I am in a low vibration. I worry about anything and everything. I only look at the negative aspects of life and that blocks me from finding clarity. On the other hand, when I am feeling creative and in a flow, when I feel free and productive, I am on a high vibration. I feel positive, optimistic, happy and full of new ideas. I am also able to project that positive energy to people around me and positively influence their day and life too.

Stress, problems and challenges never go away. We have good days and bad days. The key is to identify when we are falling into that low vibration mode and to find strategies that help us to shift into a positive vibration and back into that creative flow. It's down to us. We have the power to shift our mindset and get back into that positive vibration.

Running a business is no walk in the park. I have a great team around me but, at the end of the day, I need to step in and advise, direct and pick up any slack to keep the business moving. There are days when everything flows perfectly and days when all that can go wrong does go wrong. I love coming up with solutions and sorting out challenges and, when I am in a flow, solving problems gives me a sense of achievement. But there are times when everything is happening at the same time; I solve one problem on Monday and a new set of problems and challenges comes along on Tuesday. I meditate and try to keep my energy high but there is a point when, like everyone else, I may break. I feel overwhelmed, and feel that everything is against me and I am lifting a mountain.

When I look into my patterns, I love my morning routine: wake up early, have my hot water with lemon, espresso, meditate, read a few inspiring pages from a book or listen to something inspiring, work out. This is the morning bubble that sets me up for the day, but what I felt I was missing was a buffer between my day and my evening back home. If I had a challenging day, I would go back home with low vibration, low energy and pretty much write off my whole evening, just counting the hours until the next morning when I could once again enjoy my morning routine. If anyone asked me to do anything after work, there is no way I would do it. I was miserable, tired and no fun to be around. Was I living my best life?

Certainly not. I allowed my low vibration and energy to take away any fun from my life. As I have noted, when I went back and looked at my last year, it was clear that I was repeating that pattern. Day after day. Something had to change. I needed to bring some fun into my life. It wasn't that the opportunities weren't there, it was me sabotaging any fun in my life by projecting this low vibration and low energy, and assuming this was going to be my after-work mood so I may as well write it off and sleep it out. I realised that just going straight from work to home, I was bringing my low vibe back home with me and all I wanted to do was sit down and be passively entertained, by a boxset, Netflix or scrolling down social media.

I needed to find a way to raise my vibration from the day-stress mode to a high vibration. It didn't matter if I was going out or staying at home, I needed to start living my best life and enjoying life after work. Here and now.

So, I created an after-work routine. I'd slot in a fun workout class with uplifting music, like a spinning class with music I love, or stop by a cool new coffee shop and have a (decaf) espresso and enjoy the atmosphere and the music, or say yes to that invite or organise a fun dinner with family on a weekday, or read a few pages of fiction to take me to another place. I could go and walk into a store and wander around without a need to buy anything, just explore and look around, maybe stop by a gallery, even for a few minutes, and get into a different mindset. My mornings would be about motivation and my evenings about indulging, taking it easy and treating myself to something different: something that doesn't drive me to do or achieve anything, but fills me up with inspiration and takes my mind off the day.

Also looking at how I present myself, on days when I feel really low I try to dress better and put more effort into my hair and makeup. Going out of my way to take care of my appearance helps to lift my mood and project positive vibes. I make sure that the way that I present myself is intentional and elevated: this way I will also feel intentional and elevated. Taking care of my appearance helps raise my vibrational energy.

The way you present yourself and the way you treat yourself send a strong message to the universe. If you present and treat yourself to beautiful things and positive thoughts, the universe will bring you more beautiful things, positive thoughts and opportunities for more positivity. This is not about material goods, it is about the quality of everything that surrounds you.

Let's start with your wardrobe: do you have a wardrobe full of pieces that you save to wear on special occasions? I used to be like that and there was a point that I decided to shift my mindset and only possess and buy things that I can wear every day and enjoy. If I buy something that I can't enjoy immediately, I return it. It's about enjoying what we have now. At home I used to have some beautiful glasses and plates that I would save for special occasions ... not any more. Why can't I have my daily hot water and lemon in a beautiful luxury cup? Who am I saving this for? I was raised in a family that always saved everything for 'special occasions', but that way of living didn't serve me any more. I had to change. I realised I needed to treat myself to beautiful and luxurious things every day. I needed to shift my mindset and convince myself that I was worth all those beautiful things, every day.

Another thing I like doing is writing two lists: one with what raises my vibration and fills me with happiness and positivity, and one with the things that lower my vibration, making me feel blocked and overwhelmed. When I identify the triggers and what works to change things, this helps me quickly try to do things to shift that energy. Some of the things that raise my vibration are being creative at work, leading my team, working out at a beautiful studio, great music, quality nutritious food, a good night's sleep, a great espresso, a powerful meditation class, modern luxury, getting inspired by fashion. What lowers my vibration are things such as getting involved in dramas, toxic people around me, lowering my standards, comparing myself to others, judging myself, getting stuck in a routine that I know doesn't serve me any more. When my lists are done I ask myself, what do I want more of in my life? What do I want less of in my life? And I build my day around this.

In order to do less of the things that drain me, it's important to value my time. If I am spending lots of time on minor things that my team can deal with, then I am not valuing my time enough. By delegating and choosing to step back and focus on the big picture, not only do I empower people around me, but I am protecting my own energy as well.

Sleep and nutrition are the other big things for me. I have noticed that the days I get stressed, overwhelmed and tend to battle with negative energy are usually days towards the end of the week. This is when the stresses have accumulated and the pressures of running a fast-moving business have meant I have compromised on my sleep and eaten on the go or indulged in food that isn't good for me.

When I start the week rested after a weekend of taking care of my body, the days go so much better and I project a lot more positive energy.

Recently, at the end of each day, especially when it has been a challenging one, I write down three things that I have achieved on that day. If I can focus on those three things that I am proud of and make myself feel good about my day, I will stop focusing on any negatives or challenges that come my way. It's changing the point of view. Every day is a mixed bag of positives and challenges, and it's important that we look at them from the right perspective. Feeling good about a few great things that happened raises our energy, makes us feel positive and sets the tone for more positivity and great things to come our way.

How to Live Your Best Life Secret #9

10 ways to raise your energy vibration

You will be at your best when you are at a high vibration. You will be happy, creative and a positive force on people around you. Be conscious of your energy and find strategies and switches to get you back into that state so you can live your best life. The time is *now*.

1. Make a practice of writing down at the end of the day three positive things about the day: three achievements or even small things that you have accomplished and taken off your to-do list. That will make you feel good about your day and take that feeling forward to the next day too. Write positive affirmations. Imagine you are with someone who loves you and you were to talk to them about your problems. What compassionate words would they say to you? Write them down and repeat. Be kind to yourself, be compassionate to yourself first and be your own best supporter.

2. Take care of your nutrition. A well-nourished and rested body is the framework for a positive mind. Do not underestimate how good nutrition can shift your energy. There are times when I feel my energy is low because I have skipped lunch and I am about to go into a meeting. I give myself a break and have something nutritious to energise my body

before I go into that meeting. Low energy in the body means low energy in the mind.

3. Prioritise sleep. I used to be quite rigid with my early morning routine, waking up at 5.30am to fit in all my self-development before the day started. I have loosened it up a bit lately and if there is a day when I need to catch up on my sleep, I don't force myself to wake up at that time. I think to myself, if I do my morning routine three to four times a week, that is fine. The rest of the days, I will rest and take care of my body and instead of doing a two-hour self-care morning, I can condense it to half an hour and that extra sleep will give me all the positive energy that I need. Everything starts on the inside, and body and mind are interconnected.

4. Write down two lists, one with what raises your vibe and one with what lowers your vibe. Be conscious of when you are in one state or the other, and have your quick energy-shift strategies in hand to change your vibe.

5. Put more effort into your appearance. The way you look projects the way you think about yourself and how others perceive you. I can't say I am fully on with hair, makeup and the perfect outfit every day. I do my best to be as presentable as possible but on days that I don't feel great, I put in a lot more effort to look good as it really helps me shift my mood.

6. Work out. I usually work out first thing in the morning to get my day started on an energy high

and also to get it out of the way, but there are days that an evening workout after work is crucial to clear my head and get those endorphins going. So, keep a set of workout gear ready at work and get that evening exercise going. It could just be walking for a few blocks with your favourite playlist while you get some air at the end of the day. Make it easy.

7. Meditate. I find that when I am especially stressed out, a group meditation class at a studio is a really powerful way to get back into that positive state. Meditating by yourself can work too but I have to admit that the power of a group meditation and being in that room with a number of people who all meditate on positive energy is a lot more powerful.

8. Try to help someone. Sometimes we are all in our head and overthink our own problems. We can quickly shift the energy by helping someone in need. It could be someone we love that needs some help or we could do some charity work; helping a cause can really make us feel positive and high energy. And practise kindness: sometimes when I am in a bad mood, I go out of my way to be nice to people around me, wish someone a wonderful day, give out a genuine compliment, send out an encouraging email. This helps create a positive energetic field around me that puts me in a positive mood too.

9. Upgrade your everyday life. You don't need a whole new wardrobe, a brand-new home or something completely new and unattainable. You can find some easy upgrades in your life, such as cleaning up your old wardrobe and refreshing it with a few new pieces, or refreshing the cushions on your sofa, investing in some beautiful coffee cups or getting a luxurious, beautiful notebook for your daily notes. By refreshing your life with a few beautiful things that upgrade your day to day, you will immediately feel elevated.

10. Believe in the law of attraction. The more you love yourself and your life, the more you will attract positivity and love from all areas of your life. The more abundance you make yourself feel, the more abundance you will attract to your life.

If you enjoyed this book, then let's keep the conversation going. You can reach me on social media via @MrsRodial on Instagram, TikTok, Twitter and Clubhouse. Let's connect!

Acknowledgements

I'd like to thank my team at Ebury for believing in my third book. This is proof that there IS overnight success, after you've proven yourself the first time. I am grateful to have found Rory Scarfe as my agent. He's been the best at sharing my vision, helping me keep my cool and leading me to the right decisions. A huge thank you to Sean Cunning for helping me to edit the book and for teaching me to keep things light and not take myself seriously. My illustrator Emma Kenny for drawing the most fabulous illustration for my book cover and for bearing with me with those 1am emails when I would wake up panicked about whether we should go with the Givenchy or the Celine handbag. We got there in the end. Finally I'd love to thank my team at Rodial for always supporting me on my projects, and my fabulous @MrsRodial Instagram & Overnight Success podcast community, you all inspire me more than you would ever know.